Sustaining Simplicity: A Journal

Anne Basye

Credits

Author: Anne Basye

Editor: Rochelle Melander

Design: Kristina Meyer + Matt Fey, Orangeflux, Inc.

Production Team: Patricia Schultz, Connie Sletto

Sustaining Simplicity: A Journal
© 2007 Evangelical Lutheran Church in America.
Printed in USA
ISBN: 978-6-0002-1892-8

Acknowledgements

Thanking is a kind of infinity, with no beginning
and no end. But to single out a few folks rolling
around with me in the universe of gratefulness:
My son Alex, for his willingness to be written
about, again and again. Good thing he has a
different last name! My longtime neighbor Dick,
for all he is teaching me about aging with grace
and good humor. My parents, for making an
exception to their rule of not reading books
by their children. Every friend, sibling, or
acquaintance named or not named in these pages,
for walking with me through life. Jim Bodeen,
for photos on pages 65, 109, and 148. Dianna
Long, for art on pages 80 and 134. Colleagues
who helped bring this book to life, for their
talents and encouragement. Imagine yourself
thanked in one of the 465 languages listed on
the Web under "thank you foreign languages."
If only I could invent a new way to express it,
just for you!

Additional materials for individual and small group
use can be found at the ELCA Web site,
www.elca.org/hunger/resources/simple/sustaining.html

Contents

Introduction

People outside the church sometimes suspect that
people inside the church will swallow anything; that
our lot is to dutifully follow God's marching orders,
without ever questioning them. But I've found the
opposite is true: it's faith that gives us permission
to engage life's important questions and faith that
equips us for the struggle.

As a small child, I knew all about God. I knew where
he lived: behind the wall above the sacristy, just to
the right of the altar. I knew what he looked like:
old and grizzled, with a white beard and a long white
robe. I knew what he wanted me to do: pay attention
in religion class, mind my parents and grandfather,
and be a good older sister.

Adolescence replaced my early certitude with all
manner of questions: Where did the world come from?
Was God really a boy? How should I live? Like Jacob
and his angel, I've been wrestling ever since. When
one question was answered, another one appeared. The
last fifteen years or so, my biggest question has
been, "What is necessary?"

"What is necessary?" is a different question than,
"How can I spend less?", or, "How much can I save?"
Those questions help us adapt to our culture without
ever questioning its premises and beliefs. "What is
necessary?" is an exit door. It invites us to take
a good look at a concept of "the good life" that
always requires more and start considering other
sources of wisdom. Like God's maxims for the good
life, which I absorbed when God lived upstairs in my

church. Love one another. Share meals and enjoy one another's company. Practice integrity and kindness. Beat your swords into ploughshares. Care for widows and orphans. And remember to express your gratitude to your creator.

Unfortunately, this wisdom had been buried under my proliferating possessions and crowded days. Asking, "What is necessary?" every single day helped me sift through that stuff and nonsense and begin to recover those enduring principles.

"What is necessary?" inspired the journal entries you're about to read. They are not a prescription for living, but a record of challenges and choices. Use them to begin asking this question about your own life and exploring the answers fearlessly. Because our lives are not the same, your answers will surely be different. I hope you can draw some inspiration from the answers I found trying to live simply in a big city.

As you'll see, a lot of my struggles have been around stuff—a logical place to begin for citizens of the stuff capital of the world. That struggle never goes away, because every time an object goes out the door, a new one is trying to insinuate itself into my life! My struggles around time and activities also continue; I hate to refuse an invitation to a good time. But stuff and time are easy compared to the uncomfortable territory this question is taking me to now: justice. Shedding excess has made me see waste. Labor wasted in the pursuit of things with no lasting value. Time wasted on inessentials. Paper and plastic wasted in elaborate product packaging. Metal and glass wasted after one use. People wasted by a system that demands more, more, more.

It's a system we're all part of. As one economic analyst has pointed out, while as workers or producers we are "fed up and worn out," as consumers we are "impossible to satisfy." We groan about our long hours, but we want "59-cent tacos, $199 coast-to-coast flights, instantaneous delivery, a never-ending cavalcade of new products and, oh yes, don't forget 24/7 technical support . . . A chicken in every pot has become two sport-utility vehicles in every garage. American consumers have rewritten the Bill of Rights: life, liberty, and more cheap stuff."

Are we *really* about life, liberty, and more cheap stuff? Or can we stand in the confidence of God's love and question our selfishness? Might the powerful question, "What is necessary?" teach us to live in ways that help shape our culture into God's culture? That's my prayer, for you, for me, for our children.

—Anne Basye

Winter

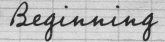

Beginning

Today I took the Christmas tree down. Putting it up is a cozy, group ceremony, with carols in the background and a glass or two of eggnog. But like the little red hen that couldn't find helpers to bake, taking it down falls to me alone.

I don't mind. New Year's Eve may be the official celebration, but this is when I feel the calendar turn over. While I'm sorting ornaments, I'm wondering: what will happen between now and next December?

Some of those answers I already know. Next December, God willing, I'll be 49. Alex will have graduated from high school and—please, please, please!—begun college.

I'll be a fledgling empty nester; 50 will be right around the corner.

Packing away the tree-top star—yellow construction paper, stuck all over with red and green star stickers, "Alex" scrawled across the middle—I realized that much of my life is about to be dismantled. Carpools, school buses, PTA meetings—it's all history. Alex will soon be minding his own affairs, with minimal assistance from me. Turning 40 was comparatively easy. Alex was 9, and I was in the middle of mothering. Small things changed all the time, but basically life was about maintaining continuity: working, volunteering at school, driving Alex to baseball games, helping him with homework, cooking supper, doing the laundry. Forty was a landmark, but no reason to set out in a new direction.

Now we're *both* searching for new directions.

I do have a good handle on who I am today. I'm 48 and divorced. Mother of a 17-year-old high school senior. Owner of a two-flat apartment building in Chicago. Daughter, daughter-in-law, sister and sister-in-law. Friend and neighbor. Dog owner. A writer who spent 13 years working from her basement and now earns her living as a writer for her church denomination's central office. And a woman who has learned to live simply in the fabled school of hard knocks.

Lessons on simplicity helped me prune and simplify my life into a shape that I like, into a shape that fits my values. Presuming that God wants us to make the most of ourselves and our talents, I think God likes it, too.

That shape is something I can sustain, financially, emotionally, and physically. Of course the struggle and pain of being human are always present, but there's usually enough money for the month, and I don't sit up late worrying about this house of cards collapsing, the way I used to. I'm susceptible to worry and stress, but it's manageable.

Life is good, really. There's a lot to savor and be grateful for. Maybe by the time the Christmas tree goes up again, I'll have a clue about what the next phase will look like.

Maybe.

Amish

"Oh, I get it—you're Amish," a date once said. He couldn't believe I had no car, no DVD player, and no microwave.

I'm not Amish, but I do try to live simply. Most people don't notice, because I dress and act like everybody else: I hold a job, raise my son, see friends and family, clean my house, tend my garden, and go to church.

The Amish part comes in what I own, how I spend, and how I use my time. I try to keep my possessions to a minimum and don't like adding more.

I try to track my spending and consciously make it match my priorities.

I try to spend my time on activities I'm passionate about. "Killing time" is not for me.

Life experiences, lots of reflection, and the gospel have weaned me from many of the "shoulds" American culture imposes on our lifestyles:

You should own a car, preferably two.
You should shop often; it's fun and supports the economy.
You should have several credit cards because debt is good.
You should replace your appliances often with the latest models.
You should own your own tools and appliances, because sharing is too much trouble.
You should work long hours and make lots of money.
You should rely on yourself, because no one else will help you.

I've learned that it is possible to construct a life that has depth and meaning—even without a microwave.

Venetian Blinds

Every story starts somewhere. Mine starts with Venetian blinds.

It was one of those years when Lent really felt like Lent. Not every Lent does. Some years, I'm too cheerful to embrace the discipline of walking with Jesus for 40 days. But my husband had moved out eleven months before.

Rejection stung, but shame felt worse. On both sides of our family tree, you had to go pretty far out on the branches to find a divorced person. Between the two of us, there was not one divorced parent, aunt, uncle, sibling, or first cousin. Only my second cousin had actually terminated a marriage. This was not ground I wanted to break.

On forms for preschool or doctors, I checked 'married.' 'Separated' was a word that I couldn't say out loud. 'Divorced' was more than I could imagine.

That Lent I was in a fog that sealed me off from everyone and everything. I couldn't get close to people and I couldn't let them get close to me. In conversations, I couldn't think of what to say or ask next. In some ways, I was banishing myself from everyone—and not just for 40 days.

Cleaning helped. When things are spinning away from me, a dust rag and a vacuum will restore my sense of control. Dusting, scrubbing, and sorting help me reflect while I create order around me. That's why Good Friday found me on my hands and knees with a bucket of water and a sponge. Spending a few hours in that posture of surrender, I began to accept all that had been happening. The fog of shame and humiliation began to part, and I saw ...the Venetian blinds.

Those blinds had been in the dining room windows since way, way before we moved in. They were so much a part of the building that I hardly noticed them. But suddenly they struck me as out of place. They were part of somebody else's life, not mine. They weren't even part of my vanishing marriage. They had to go.

I put down the sponge, got off my knees, fetched a ladder and a screwdriver, and started to unscrew them.

Taking down the blinds was the first step in healing. As the light poured in, I knew that my marriage was over. For months, I had been frozen—keeping everything around me the same, hoping that we would reconcile and that my husband would come home. Now my job was to make what had been our home and our life into my home and my life.

Two years later, when the divorce was final, my shame had subsided. I was divorced, not damned. When I felt bad, I just thought of what Whoopi Goldberg once said, "Normal is just a setting on a washer."

A glimpse of the
Venetian blinds

Making Space

One day the blinds seemed like part of someone else's story. The next, everything else in our home seemed foreign.

For the first time, I looked at our possessions and wondered how they got there.

From my ex-husband Max's deceased grandparents, there was a beautiful but threadbare Chinese oriental rug, a maple bedroom set, a chenille bedspread, and an ornate Victorian plant stand.

There were items from garage sales: a slightly warped ping-pong table. A classroom world map. A rickety table that served as my desk.

A rowing machine. An elbow lamp. Posters that we had framed—one of Clint Eastwood, another of a carrot. Odd wedding presents, like a horrible cut glass lamp. Two decades of National Geographic issues.

At some point, each item had been wanted. Now it all seemed like flotsam and jetsam—stuff that had accumulated around our marriage. I held up my hands and said no. No new stuff, until I understand what's here and why.

Eventually, many items went back to Max and his family. Other things I gave away. There was enough extra stuff to stock two garage sales. What seemed useful, I kept.

Next, I turned my attention to the house itself. With the help of friends and siblings, I stripped and refinished wood and fixed plaster. My sister shipped Alex a wonderful garage sale find—a charming little bed with a nautical theme. I painted its wooden rope trim and rudder a wonderful blue. The dingy beige walls of the basement I repainted a dazzling white.

In retrospect, I can see that sorting stuff was my first step in trying to make my life fit me instead of conforming to someone else's idea of who I should be. Not that I had been ceding major life decisions to others. No. I chose a college, a major, a career, friends, and a husband. We chose a house and had a child. But then things just started to... well, pile up. Divorce made me look at the pile.

Seen in the alley while walking our dog, Barks:
- A Christmas tree, in stand, with lights
- A new plastic Christmas tree stand, price tag still on
- A 5' tall, metal CD storage rack
- Two white presentation binders (I brought them home)

- A futon and frame
- Brand new package of foam insulation for water pipes (I brought it home)

Sugar Bowl

During the 'DINK' phase of our marriage—double income, no kids—money was never an issue. We paid our bills and put the weekly cash in a sugar bowl. I tracked check and credit card expenses. But where $6000 in cash went each year...groceries? dry cleaning? beer? cab fares, since we didn't own a car?...didn't concern me.

At Christmas we were generous, but we didn't spend lavishly on ourselves. Our wedding was homespun and our honeymoon was tacked onto a business trip. We bought a little furniture, but our wedding took care of appliances, cookware, and silver. We traveled and went to plays, but rarely to restaurants or movies.

When we felt we needed something, we bought it: a mattress, a sofa and love seat, a used car, and our two-apartment building, which we bought almost by accident, one Saturday afternoon. The rent from the upstairs unit was nice, but it seemed more like mad money than income. Once, debating whether a particular Cubs player would make the starting lineup, Max bet a month's rent on the outcome. Our tenant guessed right and got the month free.

Money tightened when Alex was born. When we established separate households, there wasn't enough. I gasped the first time a check bounced. How could this happen after years of responsible banking?

I felt a general worry about money and cut back on spending, but didn't take any drastic measures.

Then, five years after my divorce, I fell in love with an old boyfriend from college. Quickly we married. Quickly we divorced. Four months from wedding to separation—it was shocking and humiliating.

Recovering from my first divorce meant recovering from shame and learning a new way of seeing myself that didn't hurt. Money's role was a small one because even at our rockiest, Max and I tried to make decisions about money that were beneficial to us and our son.

This time, money problems exploded with the marriage—abruptly and violently. And when I tried to fix things, I couldn't. Although my home was my very own, non-marital property, I couldn't borrow against it without a quitclaim deed signed by a man I had been married to for only four months.

Sharon

In the middle of those dark days, my friend Sharon offered a lifeline. A few months earlier, Sharon had survived a terrible car accident that killed her husband. Besides caring for her own children and an elderly father, now she was contending with insurance companies, criminal and civil cases in the distant county where the accident happened (caused by a drunk driver, of course), disgruntled step children, and a grieving mother-in-law. To handle it all, she had quit her job.

Sharon's grief group led her to a meeting of people interested in simplifying their lives, and that's where she learned about a new study group forming around the book, *Your Money or Your Life* by Joe Dominguez and Vicki Robin. "Let's go," she said. "Absolutely," I replied. Like two people clinging to a branch in a flood, we stuck with the group for a year, trying to bring some order back to our lives.

Your Money or Your Life: Transforming Your Relationship with Money and Achieving Financial Independence lived up to its title. What it taught me was profound: I began to understand how our culture views money, and how I saw it. My attitude toward money had developed in an offhand sort of way. Shining the light into that corner gave me enough distance to look at my attitude and examine how consumer culture influenced my spending. Then I could begin trying to make my spending match my values.

It was a little like encountering the gospel for the first time. Of course, growing up in a Lutheran church, the gospel came with the drinking water. I took both for granted.

This was more like a collision. Chaos and heartbreak opened me to the possibility of change. The *Your Money or Your Life* study group embraced new habits that got us further out of, well, out of our financial darkness, anyway.

That year I started to record nearly every expense—a habit that is now ten years old. Like the piles I could see when I started cleaning, tracking showed me where my money was going. Seeing where the money went made it easy to see what I didn't need and where I could make painless cuts in spending. I canceled cable, which I hardly watched, drove less, got a programmable computer-driven thermostat, and changed my grocery shopping tactics. I also learned the skill of looking for alternatives wherever I could.

Eventually I was able to get my estranged husband's signature and borrow a little money against my building to pay the bills. I got that divorce, and Alex and I benefited from some counseling. After a year or so, things began to look better.

Bike

It was cold when I rode my bike to the bank this
morning, but not frigid, slippery, or dangerous.
"On a bike in this weather?" the teller asked me,
a little incredulously.

I appreciated the sunshine and the exercise, both
welcome on a day I'm spending indoors, working.

Sorting stuff helped me ask why I owned certain items
and how much I really needed. Tracking expenses tutored
me in sifting needs from wants and understanding the
real consequences of spending. But it was selling my
car that *really* liberated me.

Giving up a car is an act of imagination. When you
resolve to see through something besides your
windshield, you start remembering all the other ways
to move around in the world: buses, trains, bikes,
taxis, carpools, and even your own two feet.

Alternatives are hard to imagine if all you do is drive.
Back in high school, a girl friend confessed to me that
she had never been on public transportation. It was a
world she had never visited and couldn't imagine.

Living without a car in our society is akin to saying,
"Look, Ma, no hands!" It's dangerous, really. Once
I figured out I could actually live without a car,
I started to wonder: what other necessities might not
be so necessary after all?

Swap

Martin Luther King Day. My friend Nan and I took a vanload of kids to the Field Museum to hear a reenactment of King's "I Have a Dream" speech. Both of us have exchange students from Brazil staying with us this week—Karen, at her house, and Deise, at ours. The girls are thrilled to be attending American high schools. When Alex took them to a school dance, they thought they had died and gone to heaven.

Because we live so close, Nan and I are swapping cooking duties. Tonight Nan cooked Brazilian food that she learned to make when she was in the Peace Corps. Tomorrow, I'll make spaghetti.

"Swapping." Such a quaint word.

Swapping seems to have fallen out of favor. Today, everything either has a price or no value at all. Items with value turn up at garage sales or on E-bay. What's too much trouble to sell ends up in the garbage.

Years back, my former tenants and I cooked for one another on alternate Tuesdays. Their two tiny children adored Alex and loved eating with us. I did, too. Jean's Iowa comfort food—pork chops, mashed potatoes, and gravy—made every other Tuesday something to look forward to. What a privilege to walk upstairs at the end of a long day and sit down to a home-cooked meal.

I've swapped laundry privileges for all manner of benefits. In exchange for using my washer and drier, Jean and Brian kept me supplied with compact fluorescent light bulbs. When they moved away, my next tenant paid for laundry by having the staircase to her apartment plastered and painted. My artist friend Dianna painted several rooms in exchange for laundry time. For helping out with our dog when we're gone, our tenants get a credit against their rent. The discount matters to my current tenants Alison and Mary, who are very young and in their first jobs.

Swapping underwrites our skiing habit. When we were cross-country skiers, a Saturday in the woods cost almost nothing at all. But when Alex discovered the thrill of downhill skiing, I became a bus supervisor for a ski club. It's work: I have to count money and kids; shuttle the new ones to lessons; facilitate friendships among kids from different schools; get them back on the bus on time and count heads to make sure no one is left behind; and make sure kids go home with the right skis and the right parents. In exchange Alex and I have free memberships, and he pays half-price for bus, lift ticket, and lesson. I don't pay anything at all and use equipment (extremely good equipment) borrowed from other supervisors with a basement full of gear.

Alex loves skiing and he hasn't minded having me along. Ski Saturdays have been a highlight of the last five years. We've learned together, talked a lot on the ski lift, and made new friends. All because we're willing to swap.

Deise and Alex

Procrastination

Last Saturday, as all the Chicago families were meeting their Brazilian teens over bagels and coffee, Alex looked at me and asked, "But Mom, what about my college applications?"

"What *about* your applications?" I replied.

"Well, they're due today."

"They're not in the mail yet?"

"Well...I have a little left to do."

I was fuming. The plan called for host families and exchange students to take a walking tour of the Loop, lunch together, see more of Chicago, and then rendezvous for dinner. But now we were going to have to go home because Alex was dragging his feet on his essays.

It was inconvenient, to say the least. Not owning a car is terrific when I can plan ahead. But handling a last-minute crisis is harder. How, exactly, were we going to get home, finish the work, get to the 24-hour main post office, and catch up with everyone else?

We ended up leaving our exchange student Deise with Nan and family, and taking the train home. Alex worked a couple hours and then we took the train back downtown. It was bitterly cold as we walked to the post office. There, of course, we had to wait in line to weigh, stamp, and register the applications. (But thank goodness there is a 24-hour post office, or my procrastinating teen would be out of luck.) Luckily we were able to hail a taxi whose driver had stopped by to mail a few items, and he took us to the Hard Rock Café.

It was quite a journey—not the way I had planned to spend the day, anyhow. I relaxed when we finally joined the others. It was our first visit to the Hard Rock Café, so Alex and I were as wide-eyed as the Brazilian girls.

Martha

Ski day. Piles of new snow made skiing fun but the trip home a crawl. Most of the kids play with cell phones or iPods on the ride; some watch the videos we show. Some still appreciate simple horseplay and old-fashioned jokes. This morning, they saw shapes in the sky. There's a whale! See the eagle, right in the middle? No, it's a dolphin! It was downright quaint for children who have everything. My charges— the pampered children of the elite.

On the ride I checked in with Martha, my friend and fellow bus supervisor. She has a hard life, 21st century style: She lives in Chicago, works in California, and spends a lot of time on airplanes. Her husband picks her up from the red-eye at 5:00 a.m. Saturday, and drives her straight to the ski bus meeting area. Tonight they'll go to the symphony. Tomorrow she'll rest until her evening flight back to San Jose. By next weekend, when she returns, she'll have visited several more states.

She'd like to change jobs, but she has changed so often that she needs to stay put for awhile and stabilize her resume. Meanwhile, part of her likes the stimulation of all that travel and responsibility, but most of her is drained. It's hard to keep up her marriage, much less her friendships. The ski club, our community singing group, and their symphony tickets are all that connect her to her life here. When her daughter finishes college and comes home this spring, she'll want to be here more.

It all seems so rickety, so unsustainable. How many years can a person work this hard, missing family and friends, placing her own health at risk? Martha knows she needs to get more exercise and lower her blood pressure, but there's no way she can do it while she's living this way. She worries me.

My life is a thousand times easier, but I'm finding it hard to stay connected, too. Since I went back to working in an office, my connections with neighbors and community have been fraying. I used to be the queen of breakfast. At least twice a week, after Alex had left on the school bus, I would join someone for eggs and coffee. (Going out for breakfast is cheaper than going out for dinner.) In those days my definition of friend was "someone I have breakfast with."

If I used that definition today, I'd only have three friends.

Making and keeping friends takes time. Like Martha, I'm too busy to nurture my network the way I used to.

Stina Kajsa

Stina Kajsa was a fine woman—the kind my grandfather loved to praise.

"Swedish girls were clever," he said. "They always found jobs as soon as they got here and they found fine husbands—unless they were stuck up."

Stina Kajsa, my great-great grandmother, crossed the plains with her iron frying pan and settled right down to work on her homestead. (She wasn't stuck up; she was already married.) She wouldn't spend a dime on herself. She mended her clothes until they reached the ragbag. Her cooking was hearty but dull. She was the anti-hedonist.

All through my childhood, Stina Kajsa's portrait scowled down at me from the staircase wall. Her husband Jonas, my great-great grandfather, scowled next to her. The next generation of photos is slightly less intimidating. In their confirmation photos, my grandfather and his brothers are grim, but not fierce. It's all smiles now, in portraits of my siblings and me, snapshots of our children that go in my annual Christmas letter. Still, the Stina Kajsa influence—the expectation that life truly is a vale of tears, and there's no point in smiling—is still bubbling away there in our DNA.

Whenever I confuse simplicity with stinginess, I know I'm being Stina Kajsa. When stress and chaos make me clean and sort too hard; when I look at things not with appreciation, but with an eye to what I can get rid of; when I stand in front of a grocery shelf wondering whether I should splurge on sun-dried tomatoes or just get lentils—that's when I'm Stina Kajsa.

Stina Kajsa is the skinniest, meanest part of me who thinks no money should be spent and nothing should be enjoyed. When she turns up, I know it's time to lighten up and buy the darn tomatoes.

Stina never expected good times: just more snow, more rain, more drought, and more bad news from the bank. Her faith taught her to pass up earth's pleasures and wait for the great hereafter.

K. F. Karlsson MELLERUD

Lydia

Lydia would definitely buy the sun-dried tomatoes. The whole shelf!

Lydia is tall and statuesque. Her hair is dark and thick and curly and she moves gracefully on and off the dance floor. She embraces life. She's generous and makes her choices in a spirit of abundance, not scarcity.

Sadly, Lydia is not my relative. I was thinking of Old Testament women when I invented her: of Miriam dancing after the Israelites crossed the Red Sea. Of Esther, unafraid to win the beauty contest that won the king and more than equal to the task of convincing her husband to free the Jews.

When Stina Kajsa threatens to get the upper hand, I call in Lydia, spokeswoman for abundance.

Lydia's life is simple, too, but when she cooks, she skips measuring and just tosses in copious amounts of whatever is delicious. Where Stina sits inside her narrow life and calls it the only—no, the *best*—way to live, Lydia joins the dance and enjoys it without judgment.

Stina, Lydia: I need them both. I need Stina to remind me of all that I don't need, and to give me energy for big tasks. And I need Lydia to remind me that not all of life is about effort, and it's fine to stop trying so hard and sit down and enjoy a glass of wine with friends, with crackers topped with sun-dried tomatoes.

Seen in the alley while walking Barks:
- Blue wicker chair
- A blue armchair with denim upholstery and wooden legs
- A pink and red area rug, too filthy to really see its pattern
- A box of baskets
- A roller suitcase with a luggage tag still on it

Track

When I got to my early-morning Spanish lessons, my teacher Raul said (in Spanish, of course), "There's something different this morning. You have coffee!"

Pretty observant. When I started classes last year, I often picked up a half-caf tall latte before class. Getting up at 5:30 for a 6:45 a.m. class was new to me, and I appreciated the jolt.

Each time I bought a latte, I saved the receipt and recorded the $2.92 in my Quicken accounts. During the spring session I looked at my winter spending and realized I had bought 19 half-caf tall lattes. That's only $55.48, but because of these purchases, the snacks category of my financial recap was larger than usual.

I thought about it, and cut back. Now I buy a latte about once a month, like this morning. Otherwise I wait and have my coffee for free at home or work.

Stina Kajsa's influence? Maybe. But Lydia will use the unspent $60 on dinner with friends.

The discipline of recording and then analyzing my expenses comes from my year in the *Your Money or Your Life* study group. That book took us through nine steps.

First, we had to add up all the money we had earned in our lives. Starting with my first job at an Orange Julius, I used old income tax returns and social security earnings statements to come up with a total that was pretty respectable, I thought. Then we had to create personal balance sheets that showed our assets and our debts, in order to determine what we had to show for all the money that had passed through our hands. When we shared our results, I was proud of the grand total, but nervous about what the balance sheet had to say about debt.

Step Two was complicated. We had to figure out our *actual* hourly wage. From our wages, we subtracted all the expenses we incurred by working: commuting, child care, office clothes, take-out coffee and lunches, even hiring a housekeeper or a gardener to take care of chores there's no time for. The final net—our actual wage—was a surprise to everyone in the group.

The idea behind calculating an actual wage was to find out just how much our hours were really worth—and how much our purchases really cost us. Say I buy half-caf tall lattes five times a week, for $14.60. And say that my *real* wage turns out to be only $9 an hour, not the $20 I thought I was making. That means I have to work an hour and a half to buy those coffees. I might decide that's fine. But I might decide, as I really did, that I'd rather use my 90 minutes of labor on something else.

In the group, we began tracking income and expenses down to the penny, year round, so that we could see where our money was going—and to assess whether a particular item or category is worth the time and energy we're investing in it.

Another powerful step asked us to count our possessions, to see whether what we had matched who we thought we were. Finding out how many clothes I had acquired over the years made me resolve to thin them out and give away the ones I wasn't wearing. But owning 1250 books was just fine with me.

In the end, this program's many steps were less about figuring out ways to save money (although this was a big emphasis) and more about finding ways to make our spending match our values. Our monthly meetings were about discovery and support, as we saw how we had been using our money, and made changes to bring things in line with our values.

We were a diverse group. One young man wanted to quit his day job and be a roadie for a band, but his huge credit card debt—accumulated as he added 4 to 5 new releases a week to his 2000 CDs—made that impossible. He started to mull over the consequences of his CD-buying habit. His girlfriend had similar problems. It's interesting that as the youngest members of the group—the only Xers among boomers and pre-boomers—they had the fewest assets and the most consumer debt.

Everyone was contemplating life changes and needed new financial behaviors to make those changes possible. One older woman whose kids were grown wanted to sell her house and travel more. My friend Sharon, sorting out paperwork and legal issues following the accident that killed her husband, wasn't sure what to do next. I was trying to figure out how to get divorced from my second husband and recover some financial and emotional stability.

The leaders were a couple who were trying to save enough money and lower their monthly expenses to the point where they could live on income from their savings. They made it. Now they're full-time volunteers who help other people bring their financial lives into coherence.

The expense-tracking skills I learned from *Your Money or Your Life* gave me several benefits. I usually know how much I'm spending and why. But more important, they helped me stop reflexive purchasing and create the space to ask, before I put my money down, how much I need or want the product or service before me.

I love half-caf lattes, but keeping them a marvelous, milky treat works better for me than making them a habit.

Japanese Baths

Tonight I went to the Japanese baths with my friend
Jennifer and her husband Bob. It's our favorite way
to spend a winter evening. We spend about two hours
(men on one side, women on the other, of course)
sweating and soaking and scrubbing and resting.
Jennifer and I start in the dry sauna, leap into
the cold bath, switch to the Jacuzzi, go back to the
cold bath, visit the steam room, leap back into
the cold bath, spend a few minutes in the non-Jacuzzi
hot bath, then take a break. There's a resting room,
but with the TV on it's not serene at all, so we loll
around on the edge of the Jacuzzi enjoying the noise
of water and women before we start the routine over
again. It's wonderful. The saunas and baths are
so, so hot, and the water in the cold plunge is so,
so cold.

Afterwards, we walk down the hall to the Japanese
restaurant and eat sushi and soup. The cold air
feels incredibly refreshing when we leave the
building. At home I go right to bed and sleep for
10 hours, especially if I've been skiing.

We've gone to the baths four times this winter
and will squeeze in one more visit before we stop
coming. As spring warms up, so does the water. In a
few weeks it will be tepid instead of icy, and there
won't be enough difference between hot and cold. So
even though we think nostalgically of the Japanese
baths during July and August, we'll wait until next
December before we come again. It's pretty much a
winter pleasure.

Sabbath

I'm so grateful for Sundays, for church. Without my being intentional about it, church helps me live Sunday as Sabbath.

This morning, Paul, a tenor and a high school music teacher, said to the choir, "This is the only place I am all week where all I have to do is sit."

I know the feeling. Every other day of the week is about striving: achieving this goal, getting there, checking that item off the to-do-list. Sundays are where I can sit in peace and really let go. Relaxing into the words of the liturgy, the music, and the community, I stop seeing other people as demands and can almost see them as gifts. Communion moves me to tears. God's promises, embodied in the wine and bread, touch me deeply, down in my gut, not my head. They are mysteries too deep to grasp, but somehow easy to live in. Sunday reminds me of that. Sunday immerses me in an awareness of God's love.

Our first Christmas together Max gave me a very expensive set of carving knives. To me, the gift said, "I love you and care for you." I still use the knives, but the next 10 years saw that promise frayed beyond repair. In the wine and bread, I hear God's promise to love and care for me. Mysterious, embodied in ways I don't always understand but always accessible when I kneel at the altar rail.

Coffee hour deepens my sense of presence, of being. This week it was the only place I loitered with people without worrying about where I had to be next, and when.

I go home relaxed, open, ready to recognize and appreciate God's people, God's world—gifts I didn't create and don't have to manage. Gifts that are all around me. Sabbath. Thank you.

Robes and Pajamas

I've been ignoring a big problem: what to do with the clothes I got for Christmas. They are generic, useful things: flannel pajamas and sweatshirts, sweaters from Lands' End. All nice, but not necessary.

Last time I counted, my closet held seven pairs of winter pajamas and another half dozen for summer. I also have two robes—one terry cloth, a gift from my mom about six years ago, and one Polar fleece, a gift from my neighbor about three years ago. The Polar fleece robe is dark green with red Christmas trees on it—so seasonal, I wondered if I was really meant to wear just two weeks a year. But the idea was so offensive—a special robe for Christmas?? Have we no restraint??—that I wear it year-round. My neighbor is happy whenever she sees it.

This year, my mother gave me a beautiful pleated flannel nightgown and a plain red Polar fleece robe. I love them both, but they are sitting on my bedroom floor in their original wrapping. As the owner of two robes and 13 pairs of pajamas, do I give the new items to someone who needs them more? Keep the new ones and give away older pairs? Keep it all and give nothing away?

If I give the pajamas away in their packaging, who gets them? My friends have crowded closets of their own. Maybe our parishioner who lives in a nursing home would appreciate them. Or the refugee family who came from Sudan not long ago; the mom and I are roughly the same size.

If some of my pajamas were in tatters, I'd rip them up for rags and put the new nightgown in the drawer. The terrycloth robe will be a rag soon, but I need it for July and August, when Polar fleece is too warm.

Eeny, meeny, miny, moe. I'm still undecided.

More Christmas

Then there's the purple sweat suit.

I'm done with sweats. That's all I wore during my young mom years, when I trudged from home to play group, home to preschool, home to PTA meetings. They were cozy, but I looked frumpy all the time. One man who took me out a few times asked, "Why are you hiding yourself?"

Body image, I guess. I've always gone back and forth between really big, anonymous pieces of clothing and clothes that actually fit. College was a one-size-fits-all period. In my 20s, I went for more sculpted clothes, and even had a career-woman gabardine suit, silk shirt, and floppy silk tie. When I got pregnant, I went back to swaddling. Big knit dresses and loose sweat pants worked for motherhood and were a sort of declaration of independence from the workaday world. "Hey, don't bug me about my wardrobe," my outfits said, "I'm a mom!"

I cleaned up again for my office job. I invested in better-looking glasses and a stylish haircut. My Swedish hair had gotten boring instead of blonde, so I started lightening it. I still got my clothes from resale shops, but I looked for slightly better labels. Taking Pilates made everything fit better.

I've noticed that as women age, they trade youthful good looks for style. That's what I'm aiming for: style. Not a purple sweat suit. This gift needs a new home!

Christmas Gifts

Last year, I returned the sweaters my mom gave me for my birthday and got two great-looking pairs of pants instead. And I still have a $37 credit with Lands' End.

So if I returned the robe and pajamas, I'd have a bigger credit. But credits obligate me to buy more stuff, and buying is boring. Clothes shopping is traumatic. Must be a legacy of those long-ago department store showdowns with my mom. Once she stomped off in anger while I retreated to a bathroom to sob. We made up, but you get the idea. Shopping strikes me as a chore or a waste of the time I'd rather devote to something else.

I've also thought about packing away the new pajamas and robe on the top shelf of the closet, and using them five years from now. But meanwhile, people will just keep giving me pajamas, even when I repeat, when asked, that I'd prefer chocolate, flowers, or bubble bath—delicacies I can savor while thinking kind thoughts about the giver. But that's the thing about giving and receiving. We don't get to control the experience. Asking for a specific item is not the same as gracefully receiving whatever comes one's way.

It troubles me. In some ways, the simple life is often about control. It's about how *I* want to spend or not spend my time and money, and what kind of stuff *I* want or don't want. My motivation may be altruistic—I may want to give away more money or generate less waste and pollution—but it's every bit as egotistical and controlling as a consumption-driven lifestyle.

Wanting nothing can be rude, when it means refusing the generosity of others. Moms teach us to accept presents politely—even purple sweatpants. At my fifth-grade birthday party, when I unwrapped a little box that I hoped held a transistor radio but instead held a camera, did I cry in front of my friends or show my parents I was disappointed? I would rather have died.

Manners still matter. I wrote a heartfelt thank-you note for the purple sweat suit. I'm grateful for the gift and the challenge of figuring out what to do with it. Somehow it will be useful to someone.

Vision

I love my church, but our annual meeting drives me crazy. Every year it's the same: a lot of attention to the bottom line and complete neglect of the big picture of our ministry.

Today, as usual, we combed through last year's financial summary, asking nit-picky questions like: What is this bank charge for? Would we spend less on the copier if we stopped making worship folders and went back to the old service in the hymnal? Is this electricity bill high because we forget to turn out the lights?

Like many urban churches, this one is small and struggling. The building is paid for but it's old. Last summer a direct lightning strike took out the chimney and reduced the organ to a piercing wail. The moisture problem in the wall between the sanctuary and the gym just won't go away. The gas bill is outrageous. Expenses always exceed income.

We persist, and God keeps providing. Pledges are up a little. Our new members are younger and more diverse. We've overhauled our music and liturgy and shaped services that are meaningful and exciting. During the week, a host of ministries take place in a building that once came alive only on Sunday. Children are tutored, missionaries are supported, immigrant families are assisted, the grieving are comforted—but that's all forgotten when it's time to pass the budget. Instead of celebrating, it's doom, gloom, and fears about the future.

Unfortunately, I can be just as myopic. When I focus on where the money goes, I ignore what it provided. When I began simplifying my life, I focused on what to eliminate—not what to increase.

One year, I created a sheet called "The *Other* Side of the Budget" for the annual report folder that listed what our money had paid for: How many services we had offered. How many baskets of food had gone to the food pantry. How many people the pastor had called on. How many people our heating system kept warm. How many lives had been enhanced or changed because our church existed!

My church could save thousands of dollars by closing its doors. Instead, we keep spending money in order to serve God. I'd save lots of money by dying. Since I don't want to, I want to make sure that I spend the money I have in ways that nurture my family, build community, and help support the culture of God.

The Other Side of My Budget

MORTGAGE, UTILITIES, AND HOME REPAIR...
gives four people in two apartments a comfortable roof
over their head lets me offer hospitality to friends,
family, and friends of friends

CHARITABLE CONTRIBUTIONS...
let my church continue its ministry
help the food pantry have food to give
support local arts groups.

POLITICAL DONATIONS...
contribute to our national discourse on everything
from the environment to the Middle East.

BOOKS...
support our independent bookstore and some
talented writers.

GROCERY, MILK, AND HEALTHCARE EXPENSES...
keep us healthy

SCHOOL FEES AND FUNDRAISING...
contribute to Alex's education
help his high school educate 700 city teens

TRAVEL COSTS...
connect us to family on the West Coast

TAXES...
let me rely on letter carriers, public schools,
libraries, garbage pickup instead of delivering letters
myself, educating Alex at home, buying all my books,
and burying or burning our garbage in the yard!

DOG FOOD AND VETERINARY CARE...
sustain Barks's life so we can enjoy one another's
companionship, and I can count on his vigilance when
I'm gone.

Abercrombie

My nieces and nephews in the suburbs adore clothes from American Eagle and Abercrombie and Fitch. Alex and his friends couldn't care less. Sometimes I jokingly call his high school the Abercrombie-and-Fitch-free-zone.

"How come you're not into brand-name dressing?" I asked.

"I think it's because you and dad never cared about brands," he said. "Dad always shopped at Sears, and you just *never* shop. You never made a big deal about them, so I don't either. And you also taught me to think for myself," he added. "When thinking for myself, I don't let Nike think for me."

Then I asked why teens get so excited about brands.

"Well, clothes are where they have the greatest ability to exercise any amount of choice," he replied.

I guess that's true. They can choose their clothes and decide whether to go to McDonald's or Taco Bell.

Who pushes them into superficial choosing, parents or the culture? Does our society make us over focus on one brand versus another, or does magnifying a tiny decision somehow help us handle our anxiety about the truly big choices?

Anyway, about clothes. Alex's aunts got him an American Eagle shirt for Christmas, and, since he won't wear it, he's giving it away. It's going to Goodwill, where it will make another kid very happy. His Christmas gift problem is solved.

Closet

During coffee hour after church my friend Eliza told me how she hired a professional organizer to put her clothes closet in order. "When she was done, I had 21 bags of stuff to give away," she said. "That was three years ago. Now it's overflowing, and I need to call her back again."

Salvation Army

The Salvation Army has clever signs on the el platforms—paid for by a sponsoring bank, of course. They're close-ups of clothing, with copy on the label. So the label on a bright red, blue, and yellow sweater reads, in display type:

"If you were an accomplice in '80s fashion, it's time to destroy the evidence."

The smaller copy on the label reads:

"If you have winter clothing you're not proud of, please donate to the Salvation Army. If it's warm, we want it."
At another station is a close-up of a military camouflage ski parka. The ski lift ticket on the parka says, "You're not 18 anymore. You're not even 28 anymore." and then repeats the donation line.

I laughed, but the ads bother me. Do we only give away clothing we're ashamed of? And do we assume that poor people will like the stuff we hate—our fashion don'ts?

There's a dark side to the cheap clothes found at Salvation Army and Goodwill. That so much is available for a dollar or two says to me that we make and buy too many clothes. The used items of clothing that get shipped overseas in bulk, I hear, insult the locals somewhere else. I read an article that claimed that most of the used clothes that Americans shipped to Asia after the tsunami were burned as fuel— because about 10 miles inland, generous residents of India, Sri Lanka, and Thailand were purchasing and donating new, locally made clothing that was more appropriate to the culture.

I know a seamstress who objects to cheap clothes, new or used, because she believes that when we run out of countries willing to produce our clothes for almost nothing, prices will leap—and we will have forgotten how to make them ourselves. To her, sewing and mending are all about practicing self-sufficiency in a culture that says, why bother if I can get a new shirt for $10 and a used one for $2?

"Life truly is a journey, and the less baggage we carry the easier the ride."
—Wally (Famous) Amos

College

Letters from colleges are arriving—exciting, except they're only confirmations of the applications Alex sent off in January.

I'm nervous. Alex is capable, but these are very competitive schools. He decided where to apply and he'll decide where to enroll—but he can't decide who accepts him. Time to start praying!

The financial aid forms due this week have me all stirred up. It's partly because Max and I are deciding who will be listed as Alex's custodial parent. Since Alex splits his time between us, either one could qualify. Max says there's nothing personal, and we should choose the one that is more advantageous for Alex. But it makes me defensive—the idea that someone would think I'm *not* a custodial parent. And it hurts!

The forms seem so judgmental and intrusive. Someone somewhere is going to grade *my* financial status. The supplemental forms for the non-custodial parent probe our legal agreements. Questions about child support awaken old resentments. Questions about assets and liabilities awaken old fears about "enough." Can a college reject a boy because his parents didn't prepare adequately? Is there enough for college?

Tightwad

When Alex vacuumed the front rooms tonight, we could tell it was time to change the bag.

He groaned, because he knew what I was going to do next: cut open the old bag, empty the dust in the garbage can, roll up and staple the bag dozen times, and put it back into the vacuum once more. (*Only* once more. Never twice, or we'll wreck the motor.) Ready to roll!

I learned this trick years ago from *The Tightwad Gazette*, the newsletter published in Maine by Amy Dacyczyn. *Your Money or Your Life* helped me see money in a new way. *The Tightwad Gazette* helped me find new ways to save it.

Amy Dacyczyn devoted herself to finding ways to live less expensively. As the newsletter's editor, it was her full-time job to calculate the savings of a technique like vacuum cleaner bag recycling. "Is this nitpicky money saving idea worth your time?" Dacyczyn asked in an issue in the early 1990s. "I can recycle a bag in under five minutes including refilling the stapler. In theory I could recycle 12 bags per hour. The last time I bought bags they cost 85 cents each. So this effort is worth $10.20 per hour.

For me to net $10.20 per hour by working outside the home I would have to earn close to $20 per hour, figuring in childcare, gas, taxes, etc. Granted, I do not spend my days recycling vacuum cleaner bags, but I do fill them with ways to economize."

From my mother I inherited high standards of cleanliness and order. When I was married, I liked figuring out ways to keep things neater, cleaning more thoroughly, and storing things more efficiently. So I felt right at home with Amy Dacyczyn. Working at home, I had lots of time to follow her example. I enjoyed scanning my life for areas to change.

A big thing I absorbed from Amy Dacyczyn—and from *Your Money or Your Life*—is the importance of looking for new ways to meet needs that don't involve money. Sometimes, that means making something yourself. Sometimes it means sharing a tool with someone else instead of buying your own; taking advantage of common resources like libraries and public swimming pools; or concluding that something just isn't necessary.

That's still my favorite. Deciding *not* to buy is the best way to be simple. At the top of *Your Money or Your Life's* ten sure ways to save money is: Don't go shopping.

Don't go shopping! That really liberated me. No longer did I have to pretend to shop for pleasure. Now all I buy is the occasional book, but thanks to Amy Dacyczyn, I go to the library more often than the bookstore.

In the alley this month:
- Two mattresses
- Two sofas
- <u>Charming Billy</u> by Alice McDermott (it turned out to be a good novel)
- An off-white satin armchair, arms trimmed in wood
- A dozen perfectly good men's collared, nice dress shirts from Ralph Lauren and Alexander Julian (I washed them, kept two for Alex, and delivered the rest to the resale store)

Tuna Casserole

Tonight we ate tuna casserole, made on the stove top instead of the oven. The recipe is from a friend at church: you chop and sauté the onions in a frying pan, then add a 6-ounce can of tuna. Meanwhile, mix 3 cups of milk and a can of cream of mushroom or celery soup in a separate bowl. On top of the tuna and the onions (and maybe some sliced mushrooms, if you have a can), stack a bunch of egg noodles. Then dribble the milk and soup all over everything, turn it down and stir occasionally until the noodles have absorbed the liquid.

We love this, especially with tall glasses of milk. Other favorites: a stir-fried Chinese chicken recipe that uses creamed corn. Spaghetti. Soups of all kinds, although Alex doesn't like borscht. Chicken and pork chops, cooked any old way. For many years we watched "Wheel of Fortune" at least once a week, while eating frozen chicken pies with mixed vegetables.

All delicious, this comfort food.

Compost

February is not a good month for compost. Whatever I throw out— onions skins, coffee grounds, orange peels— just sits on top of the frozen pile.

Last year I made a worm barrel out of a garbage can, compost, and leaves. The idea was that the leaves would keep things nice and airy, the worms from the old compost would eat the scraps no matter what the temperature, and the lid would keep moisture out. It didn't quite work. No worms survived, and everything pretty much froze solid. At least the lid kept it neat.

For several weeks it's been warm enough to bury scraps and turn over the dirt. Now that everything has finally frozen, I'm tucking table scraps under a layer of straw. I'll dig it into the soil in the spring.

My compost factory makes spring seem a little closer. It tells me that when winter eventually ends, I'll have a new crop of compost, and will have to look for places to use it. Last fall, a lot of it went to nourish the church flowerbeds, which are really sandy. Maybe this year's crop can enrich my sandy front lawn.

Why leave stuff in the alley? I think the men who threw out those beautiful dress shirts are just lazy. But others hope their stuff will be scavenged. When I set out metal, I know a truck will pick it up and sell it to Cozzi Steel. On Saturday I set out a broken vacuum cleaner and our metal Christmas tree stand. (That fancy new plastic one found in the alley will replace it.) An hour later, they were both gone.

College Visit

We're in Colorado Springs for a college visit. Alex is staying on campus, and I'm staying with an old college friend and his family.

We started our day on the el to Midway Airport. Surrounded by skis, boots, and bags, embarrassed at standing out like sore thumbs in a car of people dressed for the office, Alex muttered, "This might just be your worst idea yet." But he lightened up after we passed the Loop, and the crowd thinned. As we traveled down the southwest side, he showed me where his crew team rows and shared what he likes about taking the orange line to practice. It was a window into the part of his daily life that I don't see.

In Denver, we rented a car. I tried really hard to find ways to get around Colorado on public transportation, but nothing was convenient or affordable. A car was the best option, even though with the extra insurance (necessary, since I don't own a car), the car rental cost nearly as much as a plane ticket.

After lunch in Castle Rock, we arrived in Colorado Springs. Pike's Peak, snow covered and beautiful, towered over everything. We bought a gift and found our friends' house. Although Mitch and I have kept up over the years, our kids have never met, and I hadn't met his wife, Laurie. After introductions, I took Alex to the campus for his overnight stay. He's very excited, and I'm glad to be spending time with Mitch and Laurie and family.

Leisure

This morning Laurie and I took a walk around the Broadmoor Hotel. Then I joined Alex on campus for lunch and a tour and meeting with other parents. In the afternoon, we visited the Garden of the Gods, sampled the mineral water in a little town with lots of springs, and treated our hosts to dinner at their favorite Mexican restaurant. Tomorrow, we'll go skiing at Loveland and stay in a motel before flying home Sunday.

This is only the second time that Alex and I have taken a trip that didn't have relatives at the other end of it. Since my divorce, our vacations have been based around family or Holden Village, the Lutheran retreat center where, as volunteers, we stay for free. I don't usually rent a car or stay in hotels. It's amazing to discover I can afford this three-day weekend.

I'm a little uncomfortable, in fact. I'm so used to living a basic, urban life that this taste of leisure—with no relatives subsidizing the trip with their homes and cars—feels rich, almost forbidden. But I remember words my mother used to say when my stingy, Stina Kajsa ways got out of hand: don't pretend you're poor. I knew what she meant. It's fine to be frugal, to live within your means, to direct your money conscientiously instead of thoughtlessly. But don't dishonor the truly poor by pretending you're among them.

That's the thing about our culture. We always compare ourselves upward when we assess our own wealth, so we always fall short. We don't look the other way and realize that even the U.S. working class are among the richest people on the planet.

This weekend is making me feel very rich. Being able to support Alex's interest in this college, to visit friends, to spend time together, to enjoy the stark red stones of the Garden of the Gods and tomorrow, Colorado's ski slopes—it's an immense blessing.

Salt Scavenger

I stocked up on ice
melter today—for free!
Walking to the bus,
I found a thick trench
of blue ice melter lining
the curb behind the
supermarket loading dock.
Looks like the store used
way too much when it
snowed last week. When
this week's rain starts,
it will all melt.

As soon as I saw it,
I wanted it, but I kept
walking. I don't have
a tool, I thought. And
picking it up is way too
embarrassing. But thrift
won out. I poked around
the street until I found
a discarded plastic bag
(not hard, behind the
grocery store). Then,
because it was early and
still a little dark and
nobody was around to
think, "Is she crazy?"

I crouched down and got
to work. Using the bag
as a glove and container,
I grabbed fistfuls.
Coming home from Spanish
a couple of hours later,
I found another plastic
bag and got more.
(This time there were
truckers watching, but
I ignored them.) All
told, I scavenged a
couple of pounds.

Of course I can afford
ice melter, but getting
it this way—"recycled,"
so to speak—means it
will be used twice.
Instead of buying more
chemicals that harm
gardens and groundwater
when they are tossed
around like confetti,
I can use my secondhand
supply sparingly. And why
pay for it, when there's
so much lying around?

I hate seeing anything wasted.

Hanging Laundry

Spring is almost here! The windows and back door are open, and the down comforters are airing on the clothesline.

Spring is an awkward time for drying clothes. During the summer, I hang laundry on the outside line. During the winter, it dries on hangers around the boiler. I limit the dryer to loads of knits that need a little fluffing or last minute loads I need in a hurry.

But in the spring and fall, I use the dryer a lot more. Clothes take too long to dry when the boiler only kicks on a couple times a day, and they won't dry in a warm spring rain.

Scones

At 7:00 a.m. I met my colleague Kevin for our weekly raspberry scones and coffee. Driving to work with him is a comfortable time to focus on the day ahead, but I miss reading the paper, which I do every morning on the bus. (News on the way to work; feature sections and crossword on the way home.) And if I ride both ways with Kevin and do no walking, I feel a little full at the end of the day. Four years without a car has built a lot of exercise into my life. When I used a pedometer for a week to track my steps, I figured out that I walk about three miles a day, every single day. My body feels different when it doesn't log those three miles.

It's funny to think I used to get up and walk for exercise! Now I walk everywhere just to get things done. I'm my own beast of burden.

Walking

Except for one or two Pilates classes a week, my three-mile commute on foot is the extent of my exercise routine. It's built into my day, so I don't have to worry about gym time, and it means I can eat more! I can always justify a cookie or a bagel when there's a special celebration in the office.

On the train there's a new ad: "Walking + Public Transit = A Healthy Chicago." Makes sense to me. The last time I came back from New York City I went straight to a party at a suburban restaurant. What a contrast between those rangy New York pedestrians and the puffy passengers lined up for the buffet.

This week folks are aflutter over a study that claims that even Americans at the top economic bracket are less healthy than Britons of lower means. In a letter to the editor, a woman raised in Scotland noted that now that she lives in suburban Connecticut, she believes that walking is the reason for the difference. She wrote, "To improve the woeful state of American health, an important step would be more sidewalks and more public transportation."

Amen, sister!

Baby Clothes

Sweeping the basement, I ran across the box that
holds the last of Alex's baby clothes. All that's
left are his first shoes, his Lambchop doll,
a frilly blanket my mom crocheted for him, and
three items from his parents: Max's blue and
white baby blanket and beige sweater and a Lapp
hat that my parents brought back from Finland
before I was born.

Practically all of Alex's first clothes were
gifts—sweet little striped Hanna Anderson
jumpsuits, a tiny velveteen suit, and adorable
little sweaters from admiring friends and
relations.

As gifts tapered off, hand-me-downs from my
sisters-in-law increased. When we divorced, Max
started buying most of Alex's clothes, although
between Christmas and his summer birthday, he
gets clothes for all seasons from his
grandparents, aunts, and uncles.

Lately Alex has taken to resale shopping. For
Christmas, I got him a gift certificate to the
best store. He bought a big corduroy jacket lined
with fleece and an overcoat. He's looking for a
sport coat now. He thinks it's pretty to cool to
shop for himself over at the resale store.

What Would Jesus Do?

For a couple of summers, Alex attended art camps that included daily read-aloud sessions of myths from different cultures. The gods of the Hindu myths were much more exciting than what he learned in Sunday school. "Why is Jesus so boring?" he asked when he was about 8. "All he ever did was throw around some tables at the temple."

Exploring that a little, we agreed that the significance of those turned-over tables was deep. Now I wonder how Jesus would regard the tables of merchandise in a mall. Would he recognize the mall as a temple of sorts—a temple that we patronize more faithfully than any church or synagogue? Would he turn some tables over?

FT CERTIFICATE

THE BROWN ELEPHANT

FIFTEEN ——————— 00/100 $15.00   7.81 TOTAL LEFT
2500 COATS PURCHASED 10/14

Recipient   From: MUM

Date: Robt O Brnth   CLARK ST
              Authorized Signature

47

Social Capital

Last weekend I chaperoned a 3-day ski trip to Wausau. Now ski season is over, and I can go back to my regular Saturday routine: lunch at Augie's with my neighbor Dick. We always have eggs, toast, and potatoes, and try to sit in the window so we can watch people walk along Clark Street.

Dick is 90. I met him through the block club, shortly after moving here. As a newcomer, every Chicagoan intrigued me, but Dick especially. Still living in the same house where he was born, he was the ultimate old-timer. Until Prohibition came, his family's brewery and liquor distribution business supplied bars all over the north side. Delivery was by horse and cart, of course. Later, Dick sold bananas and storm windows; most of the windows on our block, mine included, came from his company.

Although he never married and has outlived all his siblings, he is tremendously engaged in life—living proof that while hard work and education help us succeed in the first half of life, it's social connections that sustain us through our old age. Never mind his bank account—he's rolling in social capital.

Social capital is built through networks and good deeds. Because Dick has invested his whole life in his neighborhood, his church, and his sailing club; because he gives away every dahlia he grows; because hundreds of people have sailed with him; because he has a kind word for everyone, he is a rich man.

Although he's getting more frail, his network means he can still live independently. When his hip was replaced four years ago, he didn't go into a nursing home for rehab; he had a bed installed in his ground-floor kitchen and let his friends, neighbors, and visiting nurses help him convalesce.

His buddy Charlie calls him twice a day to make sure he's fine. Former tenants take him out to dinner. Saturday is our lunch day; Sundays, he eats lunch with his fellow ushers after church. When he comes for Thanksgiving, he brings roses.

Dick has a lifetime of social capital to draw on. But building social capital takes time. If we spend ours trying to increase our financial capital, how will we have time to invest in our networks?

In *The Overworked American*, Juliet Schor says that as people become more materialistic, they have a harder time forging good social connections. The long-term consequences, she says, include "a less dynamic and healthy social sphere, because people are less likely to have healthy social engagements and civil action."

When I worked from home, I had the time to engage in all sorts of civil action—everything from registering people to vote and teaching Vacation Bible School to running a Saturday recycling station. Now that I work in an office, my wide network of acquaintances is dropping away. I'm not more materialistic, but I'm definitely busier.

I also wonder: what happens when you change neighborhoods or cities and leave behind your social capital? Dick benefits because he has never moved. In a few years, I'll probably move closer to my parents, and I'll have to build my network all over again. It will be harder next time, because I won't have a child to connect me to the family networks of a community.

Letter

Alex got a rejection letter today. It makes my stomach hurt. My son, rejected! What if no one accepts him?

I'm ashamed to admit how closely Alex's success is tied into my own feeling of accomplishment as a mother. Like they say: you're only as happy as your least happy child. And Alex isn't happy.

From the paper: "Americans chase materialist dreams often at the expense of personal relationships and ties to their communities."

Spring

saturday, may 5, 19

Dear ingela,

we were very happy to get your postcard, since we hadn't heard from you in ... me. I was planning to write you but recieved yours first, now I will write you. (I t... one letter writing)

Its also good that you got your posters, I'm very sorry for the delay and hope ... be ripped up when you got them. (that's some thing else I put off)

After our freezing cold, snowy, and wet "sacremento winter, spring has come and ... approaching... last week was beautiful, temporying in the 80's, clear skies, a small ... backyard full of people, including the johnsons. this week has been windy and cool... up partially cloudy, and yesterday it poured for about an hour and then cleared ... is morning is beautiful. land park is full of people, and everybody is riding bicy... broken. daylight savings time is here again also, and it feels like summer. my ... I wish I was in sweden over and over again. my parents had hoped to go in septembe... re planning a trip next may... a year away. the johnsons still will go, maybe ... way in their luggage and come visit you, but I doubt it.

school is out in another month and my vacation plans are more or less made ... etely going to kennedy high school for summer school to take japanese and ... ss class, so that I'll be able to fix our volvo and station wagon, speaking of car...

Errands

Today I rented a car from I-Go, the car-sharing company. With Alex's help, I loaded up the car with all the paper, glass, and cans in the basement and took them to the recycling center. Then I stocked up on staples at the discount grocery store, visited the library, and went to the bakery thrift store for a freezer full of whole wheat bread. Toward the end of this three-hour spree, I bought 40 pounds of dog food before returning the car to its parking space at the grocery store.

It was the kind of errand day I used to tackle in my own car. I never was the kind of person who hopped in a car on a whim. In my driving days, I always tried to consolidate errands so that I got everything done in one long trip. It saved gas and time, but it drove Alex crazy. On the way to a baseball practice, I would make four stops. Once he said to me, "The problem with you, Mom, is that you always want to get the most out of everything!" I laughed because it struck me as a compliment! I do like to get the most out of everything—the most enjoyment out of every meal, the most value for the dollar. It's definitely my approach to life and probably always will be.

Groceries

I've been a fan of the discount grocery chain
Aldi since I followed Amy Dacyczyn's advice and
made a price book. It's a 3 x 5 inch notebook
with separate pages for each item I buy regularly.
For each of those items, there's a list of prices
from each store. These are unit prices, so I can
tell easily which size or store is really the
best deal. Here are my entries:

Flour

Sugar

Brown sugar

Tomatoes

Tomato paste

Spaghetti

Butter

Eggs

Egg noodles

Frozen chicken pies

Coffee

Coffee filters

Dog food

Chocolate chips

Peanut butter

Honey

Jam

Rice

Cooking oil

Olive oil

Shampoo

Soap

I don't really note prices from different stores
anymore, because the very first price book I made
in 1997 confirmed that Aldi was the best place to
buy staples like flour, egg noodles, and tuna
fish. Fresh fruits, vegetables, milk, and meat,
I buy from the local fruit market.

A price book also convinced me to drop my
warehouse club membership. The only things
worth buying were 50-pound bags of dog food,
one-gallon bottles of soy sauce, and 10-gallon
buckets of powdered laundry soap—all things
that get used up fast around here. (Okay, the
soy sauce lasts a year.) But for two of us
and the occasional guest, it just wasn't
worth spending money on anything super-sized,
especially stuff that is over-processed,
frozen, and not particularly healthy. Counting
the annual fee and the gas and mileage it took
to drive there pretty much wiped out the savings.
And now, without a car, it's not an option.

The price book also convinced me to buy whole-
grain bread from the bread thrift store. I buy
it five loaves at a time and freeze it. But
when I visited yesterday, there was a sign
announcing its closing. Another condominium,
probably. This part of the city has changed
so much, there may not be any bakery thrift
stores left. I'm going to have to rethink that
strategy. Amy Dacyczyn would recommend baking
my own bread—a lovely idea, but maybe in my
next life.

Ask

When I need something, I ask around. The grapevine usually works.

I ask for tenants—they always turn up, without advertising.

I ask for house sitters. They arrive.

I ask for rides—if the driver and I are going to the same place.

As a consequence of all this asking, I've become the give-to person. Friends think of me first when there's something they want to pass along. I've had first dibs on winter coats, books, CDs, sweaters.

After the church Thanksgiving meal, the basement ladies send the turkey carcass home with me, because they know I'll make soup. (They send home the extra foil, too, for me to recycle.)

My neighbors gave me a 6' aluminum ladder when they moved into a high-rise. For $15, I took the wicker porch furniture.

My colleague Kevin gave me an extra coffee pot, so I can make more coffee when I house his extra family members.

Asking isn't mooching. I never ask for money. Everything I ask for is on its way out the door already.

Give

Cooking a big vat of soup for this week's Lenten supper, I thought: I'm a giver, too.

When I shop at Aldi, I pick up stuff for the local food pantry.

I donate my services as church musician, substitute choir director, and Edgewater Singers' accompanist.

We have hosted church leaders from Liberia, Tanzania, Germany, and Denmark who needed accommodations during visits to my denomination's main offices. Before Deise, our exchange student from Brazil, there was Marco, from Germany. At a planning meeting for the Brazilians, an adult leader asked Alex, a little condescendingly, whether his family had ever been involved in any international programs. He was a little taken back by Alex's long reply!

Domestic visitors troop through year round. We've got beds and linen for four, plus two sleeping bags.

More goes out to second-hand stores than comes back from them.

There's cash for church and social ministries, half a dozen political causes, and some arts groups, because after all, *they* ask, too.

Cleaning

Holy Week. Time to really start cleaning: dust
ceilings and picture frames; wash curtains, walls,
woodwork, and floors; dust and polish furniture; send
the rugs to be cleaned; thin things out. All while
blasting oratorios and requiems.

Alex is an able assistant, but this year I want to get
it done in a hurry. I called a woman who cleans for a
neighbor and asked her to join me on Saturday for a
cleaning binge. Paying her to help means everything
will be done in a day.

Physical labor is satisfying, but I don't have to do
absolutely everything myself.

Rejection

Another college rejection
letter arrived today.
That's two rejections
and two wait lists. Only
one more is due.

Alex is shocked, hurt,
and confused. He feels
frozen, like he can't do
anything until he gets a
'yes.' Getting accepted
someplace would bring
some closure.

I watched a friend's
daughter sweat through
the college application
process. Just like Alex,
she received three
rejection notices and
two wait lists and was
devastated. Eventually she
was accepted to a college
she liked very much.

Somehow, this will work
out, too. Rationally,
I tell myself: those
dark hours when it seemed
Alex would never be
toilet trained eventually
passed. With practice
and patience, he learned
to tie his own shoes.
To cross the street by
himself. To use a knife
and fork. To write in
cursive. To play
shortstop. To swim.
To play the piano. To
say please and thank you.
To go to high school.
And he *will* go to college.

A sick child, a lost
child, a child who dies—
they're real disasters.
This is just a setback—
but it still hurts a lot.

No

The fifth college reported today—my alma mater.
It was a no.

"What did you do," I yelled, "write 'my mom made
me do this' on the application?"

"Well," he muttered, "I *may* not have finished
the supplemental application." Because he didn't
really want to go there, he didn't really do
the work.

So, he has three noes and two maybes. Alex is
completely depressed. His counselor is telling
him about some other places he could apply. And
for Plan B, he has inquired at a local university
that serves mostly commuters. He is also writing
letters to both wait list colleges saying why he
should be admitted. It's hard. To Alex, "maybe"
is "no," and there's no point even arguing.

I'm the same way. It's hard to persevere in the
face of a negative judgment. But the rep from one
of the wait-list colleges says a maybe is not a
no, and they want that letter.

no, no, no, no, no, no,
no, no, no, no
no, no, no,
no, no, no,
no, no, no,
no, no, no,

In the alley today:
A beautiful and delicate little black table with two folding leaves, near Dick's garage. Later, walking Barks, I saw a man taping the legs and leaves together. When I finished walking Barks around the block, he was carrying the table home over his head.

Child of God

Sunday school and confirmation taught Alex that we're all children of God, that God loves us all, that we're all equal in God's sight.

This college application process is teaching him exactly the opposite.

"The system is so impersonal," he told me. "It's just a lot of people looking at a lot of names. Where is God in that?"

Hmmm. Good question.

I know God has been present in Alex's life from the beginning, when our pastor held him and said, "Alexander Frank, child of God, you have been sealed by the Holy Spirit and marked with the cross of Christ forever." Welcomed into a community of people who accepted, loved, and cheered him on, Alex was a child of God, no matter what. But this incessant *no* from colleges seems to be trumping his baptismal identity. Mine, too. I realized this week that neither one of us had much experience with being passed over. In grammar school gym class, I was one of the last picked for any team, but in most other endeavors—college, jobs, committees—I've almost always been chosen. The last couple years of high school have also developed Alex's sense that when his hand is raised, he'll be picked.

Until now. Now we're experiencing life among the excluded. It's hard to hear God saying: "Never mind college. You and Alex are both loved, wildly and unconditionally." I'm too busy trying to figure out what this crisis is revealing about my parenting. (Is this my fault? Should I have pushed harder? Is this a consequence of years of poor communication between his dad and me?)

And the voice Alex is listening for belongs to a college admissions officer.

Thank goodness that weekly worship reminds us that we are loved children of God. God's voice may be faint, but God is still here, with us, in this moment. On Sunday I can remember that the questions Alex and I are asking are about our value vis-à-vis the world—not our value to God.

Our challenge is to keep listening to God every day of the week, instead of surrendering to voices that define us through our possessions and ambitions. When Alex told me sadly, "I'm on the edge of being nobody at all," I had to contradict him. "That's not true," I said. "The basics were covered when you were baptized. You are someone. You matter. You really, really do."

Georgia

I was sleepy and listless when I got to work today.
While I've been investing lots of night time hours
worrying about Alex, the problem, I think, was too
little breakfast, too early. On days I go to Spanish,
I've already been up and out for four hours by 9:30
am. A bowl of Cheerios just doesn't last that long.
Coffee and a slice of bread with cream cheese perked
me up. My colleague Georgia gave me the bread, with a
lecture about cutting back and resting more. "Saying
no is part of life," she scolded. "Not part of mine!"
I said. "If I say no, I might miss something."

Leaves

Last week there was a hint of green in the trees—
the merest brush of color. Tomorrow May begins,
and even the leaves of slow-greening trees like
the locust in the front yard are bursting out.
Warm winter or cold, short winter or long, this
is the week that the leaves make their debut. It's
so exciting! First, that intense yellow-green hue,
then the darker green that brings summer shade.

Crocuses are long gone and daffodils are fading,
but there are red and yellow tulips in every yard.
Japanese cherry trees, apples, crabapples, and
redbuds are flowering. Even the lilac is out! With
Dick's permission, I cut a big bunch from his
bush, and now my house smells like lilac and the
Easter lily that's still blooming.

With so much color and fragrance, it's hard not
to be in a good mood. Even Alex has cheered up a
little. To think everything was brown and boring
just three weeks ago.

The best thing about spring is that it's a gift.
It makes me think of that quote by Abraham
Heschel: *Indifference to the sublime wonder
of living is the root of sin.*

Ray

My friend John and I ate supper at Calo, the Italian restaurant in our neighborhood. I always have a plate of linguine with mussels, a glass of red wine, and salad— never, never minestrone.

That's because of Ray, a homeless man who was regular in the neighborhood for, oh, a dozen years. He visited me often and sometimes slept in my foyer. Now he lives in a nursing home, because he's too old and frail to manage life on the street. He loved living outdoors. When he lived on the loading dock of the convenience store, he would throw his arms wide and yell, like a prophet (he is almost completely deaf), "Fresh air! Blue sky! Airplanes!" and then go back to reading his *New York Times*.

Ray used to leave presents on my porch: slightly bruised eggplants or bananas from the clearance shelf at the fruit market, a white plastic tub of soup from a kindly Calo waiter. I would cook the eggplant and eat the banana, but toss the soup. Who knew how many hours it had been sitting outside?

So I can't stomach a bowl of Calo minestrone. It reminds me of those unrefrigerated plastic tubs.

Stripped down to his clothes, his shopping cart, his newspaper, and his dogs, Ray's life certainly qualified as simple. He rarely cashed his social security and veteran's checks and lived on handouts. Rereading these entries, it sounds like I spend as much time in the alleys as he used to, picking up stuff for my house, and accepting cast-off clothing and appliances from folks who know my ways. But I'm nowhere near as extreme. Ray's eccentricities were so many and so deep that most people *did* question his sanity. My life runs against the grain in many ways, but it still falls within generally accepted cultural boundaries.

I only go so far and then stop. There's a line I won't cross because I don't want to be separated from family and friends. Deep in my cowardly heart, I want to be considered well adjusted, not strange. I'm afraid I'll never be a prophet.

Ray and the minestrone remind me of the border— the line between living out my values and leaving everyone else behind.

Choices

Ray really did choose to live on the street. Even when he lived indoors, he took long outdoor vacations. When the weather was warm, he liked being on the street, making friends, hanging out. His eccentricities made people despair, but his choices were all his.

Shelter matters to me. So does comfort. I don't want to live on the street. I want to live in my house with Alex and enjoy friends, making music, reading and writing, gardening, walking, skiing with Alex, lounging at the Japanese baths, going to concerts and opera, visiting my family, learning Spanish, working at Holden, and savoring good food. And I want time to stay involved with church and community and hang out with Dick and my other neighbors.

Hmm. Basically, I choose experience over stuff. I'll splurge on dinner at the Italian Village restaurant, but I'm never going to buy a wide-screen TV.

Chairs

My chairs are back on the porch! John came over and helped Alex move them up from the basement.

For garage sale chairs, they look great. They're comfortable, too. From them, I conduct my ministry of the porch—a ministry of welcome to people passing by and a ministry of hospitality to a friend who wants to sit in the other chair and chat for a while.

Everyone else only uses their porch for entering and leaving their homes—except the Swedes across the street. Whenever Lennart suns himself in one of their white plastic chairs, I stop to visit. Now that he's 96, he doesn't get out much so he likes the company.

From now until November, when people ask where I live, I can say "the building with the blue and white chairs."

Band Concert

I'm really going to miss being part of Alex's high school.

Tonight's jazz band concert moved me to tears. The music was so wonderful, and the kids were so appreciative of the conductor, Mr. Metzger. To them he walks on water, because besides teaching, he plays in a combo, and directs music at his church. A "real musician," they say in worshipful tones. Tonight, we heard a set by the band, a little solo gospel piano interlude by Mr. Metzger (who played standing up, without music!) and a set by Mr. Metzger and friends. The kids went wild when it was all over.

For years, I've structured my life around Alex and his activities. Parent meetings, PTA, homework, school plays, and field trips have filled my days

and even defined me. I've been mom. Who will I be next?

And what's the point of continuing to live simply? A big reason I kept expenses and commitments down was to be there for Alex, at home and at school. He's almost all grown up, and I don't work at home anymore. Soon it won't matter if I'm there in the evenings, because he won't be. Time together, a simple meal, the freedom to go to a school event—everything that has been important won't be anymore.

Presuming someone admits him to college.

Stronger

Leaving church today, I whistled the sending song we're singing each Sunday in Easter. The words are by Desmond Tutu, and when I sing it I think yes, this is what Christianity is all about, this is why I believe:

> Goodness is stronger than evil
>
> love is stronger than hate;
>
> Light is stronger than darkness;
>
> life is stronger than death;
>
> victory is ours, victory is ours
>
> through him who loved us.

These words cheer me, and build up my sense of myself as a child of God so that it's stronger than any cultural voice that would contradict me . . . like those colleges.

Home

It's Monday, my day off.
I'm settled in at my
computer with a cup of
coffee. In the basement,
at home.

This was my rhythm for so
many years: get Alex to
school or school bus,
walk the dog, take a walk
myself, and then settle
into work.

Sometimes it was lonely.
In January, especially,
when it was cold and all
the neighbors huddled
indoors, the days seemed
long and lonely. I was
prone to sudden crushes
on men. In better
weather, when I wanted to
take a break, I'd always
find someone: my next-
door neighbor puttering
in the garden, or a
friend strolling toward
Clark Street.

But working at home was
the backbone of my simple
life for 14 years.
Staying home eliminated
all the stress of chores,
shopping, and cooking.
I could throw in a load
of wash and get back to
work. Start some soup,

make a call. Finish up
when Alex got home and
then get him to a soccer
practice.

"You don't know anything
about the real world of
work," my best friend
used to scold me. I
thought she was nuts,
because I had clients and
deadlines, too. But when
Alex was in the 8th
grade, and I took an
office job, I found out
she was right.

For starters, now I spend
slightly over two hours a
day commuting. And in my
job, the eight-hour-day
is indeed a myth. Leaving
at 7:30 in the morning
and coming home at 6:30
is an 11-hour day—
leaving three, at most
four hours before it's
time to go to sleep and
start again.

Adjusting to the office
wasn't easy. I was torn
between rejoicing in my
good fortune—great
assignments, wonderful
co-workers, and benefits,
for heaven's sake!—and
grieving my independent
life. And I couldn't
believe how much time

people seemed to waste. As a freelancer, I charged only for project time; in the office, I was paid for chatting around the coffee machine.

After so many years making a living at home, I could clearly see the deal that people make when they work: you give up most of your waking hours in exchange for a salary and benefits. If you're lucky, you also take away an enhanced sense of meaning and purpose. It's definitely a trade—one I'm glad to make now that Alex is nearly grown. But I worry about the younger mothers I work with. Don't they miss their little kids? Couldn't they work two days a week from home? What are their home lives like?

At first, I only worked in the office three days a week; now I'm there four days a week. My job no longer feels like another "client." Now I feel part of our church denomination's ministry. I share the denomination's goals and know I'm living out a vocation. But sometimes I look at the calendar, where I've marked off all my business trips and vacation for the year in black marker and feel trapped. Is this what I meant to do?

In the alley this month:

A typewriter stand

A toaster oven

A black elbow lamp

Four Martha Stewart Living magazines (great bathtub reading)

Big World

The downside of working at home was the size of my world.

It was very intimate—just me, Alex, and the dogs. A few friends and neighbors. Our church. But all of our activities took place within about a mile of our home. Our whole world could have been drawn on my thumbnail.

My childhood was the same way. In grade school, my map was three blocks square. As I met kids from different neighborhoods in junior and senior high, my friendships spread out and the map grew to contain the whole city.

Eventually my map included several states and not a few foreign countries. I knew I was part of a big world, so it didn't trouble me to shrink it for a few years. The second time around, my map grew with Alex.

During those years in the basement, I felt focused: on Alex, on my neighborhood, on my church and friends, on my building. But as Alex grew more independent, I grew restless. My little world pinched.

Now my world is much, much larger, and definitely more exciting. But as the joys and frustrations of my job sweep me along, I neglect my personal life. I see fewer people. Spend less time with Alex. Use my free time to clean house instead of nurturing relationships. And I hardly ever just sit and read a book!

Slow Walk

Walking back to my place from church, John asked me to slow down. I tried.

"Slower," he said. "Even slower."

Pretty soon we were creeping along as if we were in slow motion and examining details along the way: new leaves. Robins at the tops of trees. A yellow tulip against a red brick wall.

It took half an hour to walk three blocks. Amusing but excruciating!

To John, this was an antidote to my tendency to tear through life at top speed. A lesson in stopping to smell the roses, so to speak. But I *do* smell the roses. Just differently.

About six years ago an acquaintance suggested I stop and take a breath. Her advice is still on a note in my office: "Once a day stop, breathe, and reflect."

It sounded so silly— don't we breathe all day long?—but it turned out to be profound. Stopping to just breathe really does interrupt my headlong plunge. It really does bring me to my senses and remind me where I am and why.

I do Pilates breathing a few times a day. In Pilates, you breathe in through your nose and out through your mouth, usually while a teacher is chanting, "navel to spine, navel to spine." Trying to press your navel against your spine clenches your stomach and abdominal muscles. Exhaling and inhaling in this position forces a lot of old air out of your lungs and a brings lot of new air in.

A few seconds of Pilates breathing helps me get a grip on things when they're moving too fast. To use a cliché, it also brings me back to my body.

There's one more practice I do on the way to work. The idea is to take a few minutes to use each of your senses. So, walking down Clark Street, I notice everything my body could feel: wind blowing my hair, the weight of my jacket on my shoulders, the way my backpack rubs against me, how my pants hit my thighs, knees, and calves, what my feet experience as they touch the ground. It's amazing how many sensations our bodies process all at the same time! There's so much to take in, it's no wonder most people screen out nine-tenths of it and stay lost in their thoughts.

Next, I pay attention to everything I can hear: a car approaching, birds singing, a car horn, someone's voice, the squeal of bus brakes. And finally, while I'm passing the flowerbeds near the office, I focus on sight, taking in the colors and details of nature. Well, nature as arranged by a landscaper.

On the way to work, I'm a woman with a mission, always rushing to catch buses and trains and get to work on time. I don't slow down to scan my senses, but this practice does bring me to myself before I lose myself again at my desk.

Corporate Forest

A perfect spring day. At noon I took a walk
in the corporate forest—the dozen fruit
trees in front of the office. The trees,
the flowerbeds that change with the season,
the lawn, all planted and maintained by
professionals, are for decoration, but they're
still enjoyable. Under the trees, I could look
up at the profusion of blossoms, smell their
scent, and admire the tulips lining the
sidewalk.

It seemed to be snowing fruit tree blossoms
on the patio where the smokers gather. Near my
house, yellow daffodils are growing in ground
that has turned pink with petals from a cherry
tree. Even my yard has a little yellow carpet
where the forsythia has shed.

Walking Barks, two neighbors waved at me from
their cars, and on the way to choir, I stopped
to chat with the parents of one of Alex's best
friends. Our boys are our main topic, since
we've known each other since they were eight
months old. With graduation and college ahead,
there was a lot to catch up on.

Garden

In the back yard, dozens of green stalks are pushing up.
The roses have clearly made it through the winter. There
are two clumps of poppies coming up; when I tried to
move them last fall, I must have divided them instead.
Delicate little chives are ready for my salad, and the
rhubarb will be ready in about three weeks.

The beds look great, but the grass is all clover and
bare spots. Every spring I seed, but this year I'm
starting all over. A landscape contractor comes in two
weeks to rip out the grass, widen the flowerbeds, and
lay down sod. This will be costly, but the prospect of
new grass and bigger beds is exciting. Plus, it will
look nice for Alex's graduation party.

Cookies

Nothing beats warm chocolate chip cookies with a
cold glass of milk.

Alex made cookies today. When he was little, we
baked them every week. Measuring and stirring the
ingredients, nibbling a little dough, having fresh
cookies for lunches and snacks—it was a wonderful
ritual. Then he started to criticize the slapdash
way I put dough on the cookie sheet. When he was
about 12, he took over. He does it all, from start
to finish, and shapes the dough into beautiful
little balls. The final product looks like
something a food stylist created—they could be
cookies from a magazine spread!

I got kicked out as baker, but I still get to eat.
When he goes to college next year, who will bake
the cookies?

Diapers

Today was windy and warm, so besides drying a couple of load of clothes on the lawn, I hand washed and air-dried my winter sweaters, too.

I love hanging laundry. Clothes on a line always remind me of my all-time favorite poem, "Love Calls Us to the Things of This World" by Richard Wilbur. In the middle of this meditation on laundry, flesh, and spirit, the poem's speaker cries out,
*Oh, let there be nothing
   on earth but laundry
nothing but rosy hands
   in the rising steam
and clear dances done in
   the sight of heaven.*

Laundry is so pure, so simple, so eternal. Besides lowering my gas bill and benefiting the environment, hanging laundry is a ritual, something women have done for centuries.

Stringing up diapers was especially satisfying. I liked the way that a passerby glancing into my yard wouldn't be able to tell—from the diapers, the picnic table, the hose, and the porch siding—what decade they were in. It could be 1940, for all they knew.

Diapers! When Max and I brought newborn Alex home from the hospital, we put him in his crib and just looked at him. With no nurses to coax us through the details of caring for him, we had no idea what to do next. He started to cry. Just then the doorbell rang. It was my parents, fresh from their 2000-mile drive to meet their first grandson. My mother rushed in and picked up Alex. "No wonder this child is unhappy," she exclaimed. "He's wearing disposable diapers!"

While I did learn how to use cloth diapers, a supply of disposables was always near at hand. They made outings and trips so much easier.

When it comes to living simply, I cherry pick. Favor cloth diapers over plastic, but don't pretend they haven't been invented. Air dry the laundry, but when it rains, be glad there's a drier in the basement. There are no hard-and-fast rules. We get to choose.

Wine

John and two friends from work came for supper tonight. I made spaghetti, and John brought a bottle of wine made by his son Aaron. About his sons, he's one hundred percent partisan. There are no better young men; there is no luckier father; he is blessed. His enthusiasm has been an example to me during these last difficult weeks. It has helped me remember that no matter what happens to Alex, he *is* wonderful; I *am* a lucky mother; *I* am blessed, too.

A couple years ago when I was visiting my parents, John took me on a tour of Sonoma County wineries. "I've never seen someone buy so much wine and give so much away," he complimented me. I was definitely Lydia that day, making grand gestures: bottles for everyone I knew! Presenting it to friends and relatives, I felt like the richest woman in the world.

Drinking Aaron's wine made me feel the same way. Imagine, homemade wine! The spaghetti was adequate, but the wine was the main attraction.

The meal was a farewell of sorts, as John leaves tomorrow for several months at Holden Village, where Alex and I volunteer each summer. We'll see him again in August.

Admitted

One of the Plan A colleges took Alex off the waiting list. We went to visit. He seemed impressed, and I loved it too. The financial aid offer is adequate. But he's seriously considering staying in town and attending the Plan B school, which is offering him a full scholarship to its honors program.

On the one hand, he wants a good education. On the other hand, he wonders, "If I go to the fancier school, do I have to be a fancier person?" Graduating from a diverse public high school, he's aware that the private college will be less diverse and its students more privileged. Should he go there or should he attend the kind of school that his less-privileged classmates can afford? That's his quandary.

The other seniors we know have long since made their choice. I wish my principled son would decide, so we could have something to celebrate at his graduation party.

Gesture

Mother's Day. Alex and I brought flowers and chocolate to his aunts, my sisters-in-law. I like giving consumable gifts, because that's what I like best: flowers, wine, bubble bath, See's candy. Little luxuries I can savor for a long time. My sisters-in-law gave me potted annuals and hanging plants for the garden. My mother and I just gave each other good wishes. Alex is still thinking about what to get me. Really, it doesn't matter, because he's the gift.

Senior Prom

Alex was gone all night, at the Senior Prom.

He and Ben, Andrew and Alan rented a limousine, to get their dates (Crystal, Jemia, Brianna, and Alexis) to the party. Tickets were $85 a piece for the dance at Sears Tower, including dinner and dessert. ("Dessert was the highlight," he said.)

Renting limousines makes sense because most of the kids don't have cars, and they have to pick up dates all over the city. The most ostentatious group rented a stretch Cadillac Escalade, he told me, and they bragged a lot about the cost.

After the dance, the limousine took all eight to Andrew's house. "Crystal made quesadillas and Ben made stuffed pasta shells," Alex explained. "But the oven broke so we didn't actually eat the pasta."

Eventually, Ben's mom took Crystal and Brianna home, another parent fetched Jemia and Alexis, and the boys went to sleep at Andrew's. He looked a little tired when he showed up today.

Adding up the tuxedo, two tickets each, and the shared limousine, the boys must have spent about $300 each on the evening. A significant amount—yet it still sounds safer and more low-key than my senior prom at the Sacramento Elks Hall. Last night, beloved teachers chaperoned the event; parents and professional drivers got the teens around the city safely; Andrew's parents were home all night. Back in 1974, we had more cars and less supervision. We spent more going out to dinner and engaged in post-dance activities that were, well, let's just say less *salubrious*, and conducted well out of view of our parents.

A high school on Long Island dropped its prom this year because parents were sponsoring pre- and post-prom cocktail parties and encouraging behavior that ran against the school's Catholic values. The principal complained about "the bacchanalian aspects of the prom—alcohol-sex-drugs" and the "root problem—affluence. Affluence changes people. Too much money is not good for the soul. Our young people have too much money. The prom has become the occasion of conspicuous consumption—from dress, to limousines, to entertainment. . . . We are concerned about how our young people are being educated in the use of wealth and the experience of power that wealth gives. . . . The bad use of money or wealth in any form is immoral."

Parents and students vehemently disagreed with the principal and are sponsoring their own dance so the kids can enjoy this rite of passage, illicit cocktail parties and all.

And the students at Jones High School in Chicago? Yes, Alex and friends had the limousine. Crystal, I know, bought two dresses—one each for the senior and junior prom. (No limousine that night. After the junior prom, Alex paid for her cab home, and took the el back to my house.) Alcohol, sex, and drugs? Absolutely at my senior prom in 1974. Probably at this one, too, but not among these eight kids.

That Sucks

I told Alex about the high school that cancelled its prom and he said, "That sucks for the kids." Then he told me about a new reality TV show called "Sweet 16" that focuses on families that sponsor extravagant Sweet 16 parties for their teens. (Girls, I suppose. Do boys have Sweet 16 parties?) Really extravagant, he said: "like $80,000 a party."

"They are really terrible children," he said. "If someone else gets the attention for a minute, they whine. I think it's the parents' fault for putting that kind of money at their disposal and encouraging them in those ways for 16 years."

It's hard to believe that Alex was ever 8!

Grind

My time is not simple. I am a drudge, a grind.

What I've been doing: practicing like mad for last
weekend's Edgewater Singers concert; finishing a
newsletter for a client; attending Alex's end-of-
school activities; working in the yard; cleaning
the house in preparation for my parents' visit;
substituting as the musician at church; still
slogging away at early-morning Spanish, twice
a week. Oh, and my desk job, four days a week.

My life is filled with work and obligations and
lately it all seems very old and tired. Stuck in
this time-to-make-the-donuts mode, the pleasure
of everything evaporates.

Right now it's hard to imagine something fun to
do. Alex thinks I approach *everything* as work,
even my free time. My friend John says I need to
lighten up.

I'm trying. This morning I slept in, finally. Alex
was at his dad's and everything was so wonderfully
still, with no noises from the boiler—heating
season is finally over—no commuter traffic noise,
just bird song and the soft click of the gate as
my neighbor Laura came in and out of her garden.
While the coffee was brewing I debated: make toast
or go buy a raspberry scone? I bought the scone.
Now I am sitting on a porch chair writing, sipping,
and munching, enjoying the new green leaves. Trying
to sit still. Trying to be.

Ice Cubes

Alex reached in the freezer to fill his glass with ice—and came out with a handful of green and red cubes.

He just sighed and shut the door. He knew what those little cubes were. When I cook spinach or broccoli or rinse out a tomato paste can, I pour the leftover liquid into an ice cube tray. Now and then I collar all the cubes into a plastic bag. Eventually they go into soup.

I'm *proud* of my little cubes, but Alex thinks they are evidence that sometimes I take frugality too far.

Could be. Once I used a wax cereal box liner to line a cake pan. Cereal box liners make great sandwich bags but they were never meant to go in the oven. At 400 degrees, the paper melted into the cake and the cake—made with incredibly rich, boutique chocolate I had gotten for Valentine's day—had to be tossed. (Amy Dacyczyn would have scraped off the gross part and used the rest for ice cream sundae topping.)

For years I saved our old jeans: Alex's from every year of his childhood and every pair I'd worn since his birth. Despite the holes and worn patches, the fabric seemed too sturdy to throw away. My plan was to follow instructions from *The Tightwad Gazette* and make them into hot pads. What a perfect Christmas gift! Practical, attractive, and good for the planet!

Last year I looked at the stack and realized that while I'm good at using a sewing machine (borrowed, of course!) to make repairs, there was no way I was ever going to get around to this project. When I read about some ladies in Ohio who turn old denim into handbags, I mailed them all my old jeans. Anonymously, so they wouldn't send them back.

When Alex was very small, I used to bring fresh ears of corn to my former

husband's family parties.
I would steam them and
scrape them and serve
them to Alex, instead of
using baby food. That
drew some curious looks.

One summer day,
contemplating how much
water a household uses,
I used the bathtub water
to water the tree in
front, carrying it out
bucket by bucket until
the tub water was too
shallow to collect.
Once was enough for
that experiment.

Old socks. So many uses!
Great for dusting. For
cleaning off dog paws.
For sanitary pads, on
days when I'm at home.
But never at the office.

Old bags. I almost never
buy sandwich bags,
because I have a steady
supply of washed-and-
dried bread bags ready
for lunches and

refrigerator storage.
How can people toss those
really good resealable
plastic bags after one
use, when you can get
four, five, six more uses
out of them?

Right now there's a
plastic bottle of oil
upside down on the
kitchen counter, so that
last tablespoon will drip
down into the cap. I'll
use it for an omelet.

On the other hand, I'm
going to throw out the
glass jar of honey that
has turned into an opaque
concrete block. A minute
in a microwave might
rescue it, or at least
let me get the honey out
of the glass in order to
recycle it, but I don't
have a microwave. I'll
stick to colored ice
cubes.

Sod

The sod guys dug up the yard yesterday. They thought
the ground was too sandy, so today I borrowed an I-Go
car to bring home five big bags of dry peat from the
hardware store. Rain was falling, the orange spray
paint lines that show where the sod will go were
vanishing, but I kept digging. I want it to be ready
for tomorrow, when the sod goes in.

I dug in a little compost from my two big piles by the
garage, too. Adding compost has made the soil in my
beds very dark and rich. It's easy to see right now.
The dirt that is inside the orange circle looks dry.
The dirt outside the circle, where the perennials are,
is crumbly and thick.

I'm pretty muddy now. Time for a bath. Bubbles!

Shopping Cart

Bringing home the groceries in my shopping cart, I thought about my dad.

When he visits, he gets right into the rhythm of city neighborhood life. He walks to the store on any excuse and does all his errands on foot. Talks to my neighbors. Even speaks a little Swedish with the folks across the street. It's such a different life than the one he knows in California, land of long driveways and 8-foot privacy fences, where interacting with the next door neighbor means nodding politely as you both pick up the paper from the porch.

He's much more comfortable than he was the first few times he and my mom visited. After Alex was born, watching a TV news special about conditions in desperate parts of the city, he asked solemnly, "Is this the inner city?"

I giggled. Chicago is huge. Some neighborhoods are livable; some are not. In this urban village, people know one another and work together well on problems. "You live in the smallest town I know," my mother said once.

My dad bought me my shopping cart four years ago, when they visited for Alex's confirmation. We had stopped by a garage sale, where he noticed the cart in a corner. "If you're going to sell your car, you'll need this!" he said.

He was right. I've used the cart faithfully ever since.

Tomorrow my parents arrive for a two-week stay to celebrate Alex's high school graduation.

Car

My parents drove here from California in their new car.

Cars are part of your DNA when you're born in California. Our family had one for each parent. I spent hours of my early life in cars, being driven to school, to swimming lessons, to piano lessons, to church, to the grocery store—everywhere, in fact, because everything was far away from our outlying neighborhood. There was a bus stop on our corner, but downtown was too far for children to go by themselves.

When I was 10 and we moved to my grandfather's house close to downtown, I was freed. Now we lived between two bus lines and could walk to the grocery store, the drug store, the ice cream parlor, and our new school. I liked taking the bus or riding my bicycle around town. It made me feel independent because I didn't have to wait for a ride or, after getting my license, borrow the car.

I never owned a car until I was 29, and my job moved from downtown to the suburbs. Once Alex was born, public transportation was temporarily forgotten. There was so much to tote around—baby buggy, diaper bag, snacks—and the car was an easy place to throw it.

Later, I traded up to a beautiful blue Volvo wagon. It was 7 years old when I bought it and 18 when I sold it to a young man who wanted a beater for the city.

I loved that car. It got us to play dates, Little League, and soccer practices, birthday parties, school plays, and the myriad activities of an American childhood. But tracking expenses revealed how much the car cost me. Counting gas, insurance, city and state stickers, and repair, the last few years' totals looked like this:

1997: $1731.87
1998: $2133.67
1999: $2649.28
2000: $3963.93
2001: $2524.15

This is chump change to people with car payments and long commutes, but I thought it was a lot. To keep costs down, I dropped collision coverage and drove as little as possible to qualify for a low-mileage insurance discount, but I couldn't keep my car from aging. Every time something went wrong, it cost $500—and I always had to charge it. For a while there, my Visa bill was all about the car.

I loved my beautiful blue wagon, but it was falling apart. As Alex approached high school and needed less shuttling—bar mitzvahs were ending, baseball was turning into a school sport with buses, Alex was learning to take public transportation— it was possible to start thinking about the alternatives.

First, my tenant and I tried sharing her car. Theoretically, it was a good idea; she didn't use hers much, either, and since we lived in the same building, we thought we could easily check schedules and make plans.

Eventually it became clear that our views on car maintenance and repair weren't compatible. We didn't always communicate clearly, either. Her job changed and she needed her car more. In the end, our friendship mattered more than the car. I stopped using hers and joined I-Go, the new car-sharing company in town.

Now, whenever I need a car, I can rent a Honda for a few hours. Two are parked at the grocery store three blocks away. I call in and reserve the car, walk to the lot, press a key card to the window decal, open the car, turn on the key, and drive. I pay an hourly fee plus mileage. They pay gas, insurance, maintenance, and repair. It's been great.

Last year cars and taxis cost me $530.68. Bus passes for Alex and me cost another $580. The $1400 freed up by not owning a car has gone to travel, donations, college savings, and the occasional meal out.

Capacities

"Those bright blue eyes!
So alive!" my dad said
when he met Dick today.
Eggs, potatoes, toast,
and coffee, as usual.
My dad fell in line and
ordered what we did.

Dick always greets Augie,
the proprietor, and all
the waiters and
waitresses. Augie always
responds with, "So, are
you behaving?" When the
busboy asks him if he
wants more coffee, Dick
replies, "Poquito."
People who stop by our
table to talk don't know
that he can't always
remember their name!

With all of his social
capital, Dick is the
richest man I know. Why
do we define wealth so
narrowly? If all Dick had
was money, he would be
sad and alone. It's his
amazing network of
relationships that keeps
him, a very old man,
kerplunk in the middle
of life. He has friends;
a body that moves,
if stiffly; and an
appreciation and curiosity
for life. Today he
explained how he believes
people stay happy in the
long run: a person,
he says, needs to
develop what he calls
"capacities." He means
the capacity to enjoy
something—golf, family
members, a hobby. You only
need a few of them, Dick
says. His three are the
dahlias and roses in his
garden, the opera (he used
to be a supernumerary,
a non-singing extra who
carried spears and
emperors in *Aida* and other
productions), and little
kids. Every time we're
out, he waves at every
child in the restaurant,
or stops at their table
to give them a grin.

What are my capacities?
My garden, for one—
I love moving plants,
getting dirty, or just
sipping my coffee on the
picnic bench, admiring
a blossom. Music, for
another—playing it,
listening to it. Alex,
too—what a gift his
life has been for almost
18 years.

Graduation

When people ask what to get Alex for a graduation
present, I answer: money.

It sounds crass, but it will help him achieve his
dearest wish: to do nothing for the next month but
hang out with his friends. He worked hard last
summer and fall at an ice cream parlor. So why not
support a little leisure?

He doesn't need a big present. He has plenty of
clothing, a boom box, and a computer. He doesn't
need a big trip; in July, he and my brother John
will hike across the Cascades to Holden Village.
He needs time with his friends, who are about to
scatter to different schools in different states.
Hanging out is pretty simple. Usually, they play
poker at one another's houses, or have movie night,
where everybody brings a video, and they watch
four in a row. Maybe they'll use the money to order
a pizza.

The only things I hope he'll do for me this summer
are house sit when requested and start sorting his
bedroom. It's a real museum to childhood. He is
sentimental about many of its contents, but does
he really need those old athletic trophies?

Graduation Party

Alex's party turned out to be a lot of fun. People hung
out on the front porch, the back porch, inside, and in
the back yard, helping themselves to sandwich fixings,
pita bread and hummus, snacks, and drinks. The bakery
cake looked like a stack of books, the spines decorated
with the names of his favorite subjects. Mostly
grownups came—cousins, aunts, uncles, grandparents,
neighbors—because all his friends, of course, were
having identical parties at their homes.

I'm the mother of a high school graduate. Wow!

MUSIC
AND DANCE
THEATER
CHICAGO, INC.   205 East Randolph Drive
                   Chicago, IL 60601

The Joan W. and Irving B. Harris
Theater for Music and Dance

GENERAL
ADMISSION   Jones College Prep

                   Commencement Ceremony

$ 0.00 Friday   6:30 PM $ 0.00

GEN
ADM

Pause

This is the week when I can almost taste the leisure that summer promises.

Pentecost is behind us, so there are no more Wednesday and Sunday church choir rehearsals until fall.

The Edgewater Singers are also on break until September. No Sunday night rehearsals, either.

No travel this month; I'm home every weekend.

Alex is out of school and enjoying his month of leisure. My parents have finished their two-week midwestern tour and are safely home.

The busy season at work is still two weeks off.

The evenings are warm, and I can water the new sod in my bare feet. When I water in front, I can talk to neighbors as they walk by, or invite them to sit for a few moments in the porch chairs.

This is the June I long for in January. It's so idyllic.

June

The vegetables arrived today from the Community Supported Agriculture farm in Rockford that I've been part of since year one.

As a shareholder, I share the risk of farming with the farmer. If weather ruins a crop, "Farmer Joe" doesn't lose money. We don't lose, either, because he plants such a variety of crops that something is always thriving. Farmer Joe benefits by having a stream of income he can count on and no pressure at all about markets. The thousand subscriber-shareholders in Chicago and Rockford benefit by receiving fresh, delicious, vegetables from June to November. Twice a season we get together at the farm for a tour, a meeting, and a potluck buffet set up on tables that run the length of the barn.

For about five years, I've been the drop-off site for this part of town. (I get a 50 percent discount for the work—another labor-for-goods swap!) Forty-five subscribers pick up their boxes every Saturday. This morning, I swept up all the leaves and cobwebs and washed the stairs. It was exciting to see the farm's big white truck pull up around noon. Now all the boxes are tucked under the back porch, waiting for subscribers to retrieve them. Usually I hang out in the garden on the first Saturday, so I can say hello to everyone. I did greet people for the first couple of hours, but then my friend Jennifer and I had plans. She helped me get my recycling to the center, and then we walked by the lake and ate supper at a really good, really inexpensive Mexican restaurant. Tomorrow, I'll make my first farm salad.

1006

Leafing through my first issue of *Seventeen* magazine in my seventh grade home economics classroom, I thought I was holding the key to the grown-girl universe—the textbook of teenage life.

The ads were particularly compelling. All I'd ever seen before were ads in comic books and *MAD Magazine*—ads for see-through glasses, amazing magic tricks, and other novelty items. In *Seventeen*, I couldn't tell the articles from the ads. Everything was equally appealing.

The ad with the most impact was for 1006, by Bonne Bell. Copy for this acne-fighting astringent went like this: Once she had skin problems. Now she has boy problems and too-much-to-do-in-one-day problems.

As a teen with acne, I longed for new problems. Getting busy seemed like the best way to make that happen, so I joined clubs and student government. Went to summer school. Volunteered for the McGovern presidential campaign. Graduated early, got a job. In college, I took heavy class loads. Accompanied college musicals and music students. Edited the literary journal. Skied.

My pace was brisk throughout my 20s: work, more study, outings with friends, travel. Imagine, I used to swim a mile a night! After moving to Chicago, I vowed to become a citizen, so I joined the church and the block club. After work, I went to meetings. No problem for Max, because his job started later in the day and when he came home at 9:30 or 10:00 at night, I was there too, with dinner ready.

Busy, busy, busy. Fun, fun, fun. Becoming a mother was my first opportunity to reconsider my frenzy.

About a week after Alex's birth, friends from work came to meet the baby and fill me in on the news and gossip. I remember thinking: that could be Mars, for all I care. The news that mattered was in my arms.

Now, I just wanted to stay home with Alex— well, close to home, anyway. I kept going to neighborhood meetings and took Alex with me. At the end of my four-month leave, I thought: if family, neighborhood, and job are too demanding a combination, then the job has to go.

It was slowly sinking in that while every day still had 24 hours, most of those hours weren't mine. So I cut back to part-time work, and started building a freelance business that eventually let me work at home. And there I stayed—able to get meals on the table, be there when Alex had a fever, and chaperone school field trips—for 13 years.

Motherhood made me cut back, but activities crept back in as Alex grew more independent. Now I accompany the Edgewater Singers and am the assistant music director at church. I chaperone the ski club, host the local CSA vegetable drop off site, work in an office four days a week, and freelance on the fifth. My calendar is constantly full.

"I've been having such relaxing Saturday mornings," I told my friend John when he called today. "All I do is get up, walk Barks, have coffee, work in the garden, and then have lunch with Dick." He laughed out loud. My version of "nothing" sounded hyperactive to him!

Activity is my Achilles heel. I've just plain ignored the part of simple living that says sit down, stop being frantic, and get a grip. I don't really have a grip.

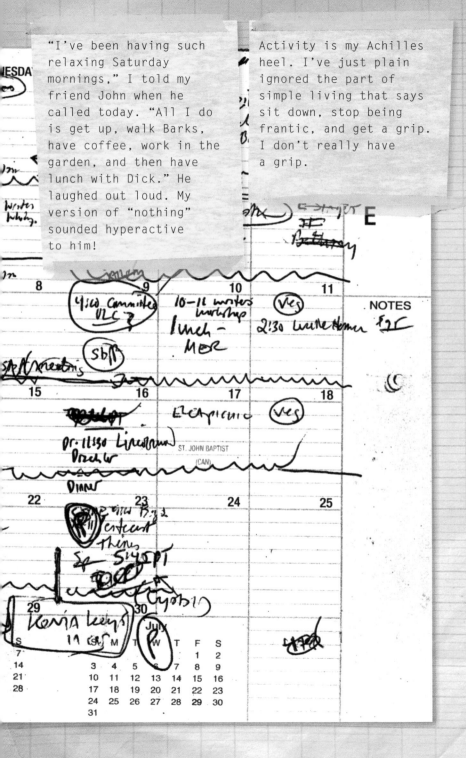

95

Dog Sitters

June is almost over, and I don't have a summer
house sitter yet.

Starting in July, I'll be gone for six weeks—in
North Dakota, Maryland, and Wisconsin, and then
Washington state, when Alex and I volunteer at
Holden Village.

Meanwhile, someone's gotta watch the dog, bring in
the mail, water the new sod, and manage the CSA
vegetable boxes from July 25 through Labor Day.

It's usually easy to find a young person willing to
take care of things in exchange for a free
apartment in a cool neighborhood. This year the
supply seems to have dried up. I'm spreading the
word, and no one is biting.

Next weekend, when I meet John in Iowa for his high
school reunion, Alex will be in charge, now that
he's more or less grownup.

Summer

www.elca.org/hunger/resources/simple/sustaining.html

I signed up to take a class in drama appreciation during school, and with all that plus things that go along with summer get 25 hours a day, but I'll have a good time. no one else in except that we have to go to washington to visit my uncle, and m Canyon, but that would be so hot!

Enroll

Alex enrolled in the private Plan A college two weeks ago. Today he withdrew to stay in Chicago and attend the local school that has given him a full scholarship.

Financially, it makes great sense. But how ironic! For all my frugal ways, education is one place where I was planning to invest the most. To me, a good education that outfits a mind for life is worth every penny. I don't want to stint on school for Alex.

I'm really wrestling with this. On the one hand, it's a great financial boon. All he has to pay for is room and board. On the other hand, I'm coming face-to-face with my snobbery. I imagine myself to be beyond the siren call of status symbols, but I want him to go to a good school and—I confess, I confess, I confess— that means name brand.

My cousin's husband once pronounced about his brother-in-law, "If he can't get into a good undergraduate program, he can't get into a good graduate program, and if he can't get into a good graduate school, it's all over."

I was appalled. How could someone be dismissed so easily or good defined so narrowly? As a young mom, I was sure that *my* attitudes would be broader and more life giving. I would love and accept Alex as he was, no matter what. And I do— but that admonishment lingers. What *are* the consequences of turning down a good undergraduate program?

I'm proud that Alex is a thinker who spends time on ethical questions, but I wish he had chosen the Plan A college. (So do my parents. They are wild with grief. Me, too.) "Mom," he said, "even with the financial aid, if I blow it, it's an expensive mistake. And can I really do the work, when everyone else said no?"

Eggs

"Fresh eggs from Amish farmers in Wisconsin, $2 a dozen."

The young woman who posted this notice at work told me that she brings 40 to 50 dozen eggs back to Chicago whenever she visits her family. "I know the Amish women and children who raise the chickens and I like to support them," she said. "Most of the eggs are spoken for, but I had a few extra this time."

Of course I bought a dozen and joined her distribution list. They are big, brown, and delicious, and I have to wash them myself—that's new to me. Buying Amish eggs at the office! Like vegetables from the farm and home-delivered milk, they offer a way I can be a food democrat, something I read about in the Heifer Project's *World Ark*.

"The typical supermarket contains no fewer than 30,000 items," says the article. "About half those items are produced by 10 multinational food and beverage companies. And 138 people—117 men and 21 women—form the boards of director of those 10 companies... instead of coming to us from thousands of different farmers producing different local varieties, these products have been globally standardized and selected for maximum profit by just a few powerful executives."

Food democracy, says the article, happens in places like local farmer's markets and community-supported agriculture farms. Growing your own (which I don't do anymore, since my job involves so much

summer travel), buying
fresh produce from local
sources—all these
delicious alternatives
"return power to the
eating public."

Sign me up! It sounds
like motherhood and apple
pie. I'll still buy
Cheerios, flour, and
canned tomatoes at the
discount store, and I
hope the supply chain
that brings fresh orange
juice to cold climates

never, ever fails. Taking
selective advantage of
mass production (hmm,
food totalitarianism?)
frees me from doing
everything myself. But
getting fresh eggs
without going to the
store, supporting real
women whose names Karen,
my colleague, knows—for
that, I'll get out the
vote.

Cone

Do the ice cream cones we ate tonight
count as food democracy? Probably, since
they came from a locally owned business
that bought the ice cream from a local
supplier. They were delicious. I could be a
food democrat all the time.

Greyhound

The poor president, I thought today, as I rode the Greyhound bus to meet John for his high school reunion: the president *can't* take Greyhound. Isolated by security, the president never really enters public space.

On public transportation, I share my space with all kinds of folks—some like me, some not. We're thrown together, trying to get to our various destinations. It's very different from a highway, each of us sealed into separate little containers, focused on private agendas, honking nastily at anyone who gets in our way.

Sharing isn't easy, and sometimes I don't want to do it. Plenty of passengers make me nervous, and some are just plain crazy. I hear more profanity than I'd like. But at least we're all there, practicing civilization.

Today's ride started in a terminal full of people that presidents and governors rarely meet or think about. Then we visited suburbs and small towns, passed farms and factories, and stopped at the world's largest truck stop in Walcott, Iowa. When we pull into Iowa City, I'll have the thrill of being met at the bus.

Not wanting to share time and space with strangers is a big reason people drive, I suppose. We want to control our surroundings and eliminate contact with the unknown, just like the Secret Service.

Our culture encourages this. We're separated by demographics and target marketing, by strategies that seek to limit certain opportunities and experiences to certain kinds of people. That public transportation reaches across boundaries makes it revolutionary. Just like church, come to think of it. Church is practically the only place you can still get to know a cross-section of the population. At my church, young singles get to know small children. The very old can have coffee with the very young. The grandchildren of Swedish immigrants share a pew with refugees from Sudan.

Church is one expression of community; public transportation is another. Both keep us connected.

Malt

Not only is Iowa idyllic, it offers ample practice in food democracy! I had a chocolate malt at the drugstore on the square of John's hometown, where all the patrons knew one another and John. An enormous pork tenderloin sandwich in the hamlet of Union. The mile-high lemon pie in Waterloo. All homemade, grassroots dishes.

Bus

Bus drivers come in all sizes and types: kind, brusque, indifferent, surly. When I get off a bus, I always try to thank the driver and wish him or her a good day—a little contribution to civil society. Tonight I got the nice chatty bus driver. "It's a good night for soup," he said, looking right at me as we came to my stop. "It is," I said, "But I'm going to make an omelet and have a glass of wine."

In general, I like riding the bus. I can read the paper to my heart's content, finish the crossword puzzle, and do a little eavesdropping on the human condition. Two days ago, some men in the back of the bus were advising a younger man who had moved to Chicago to live with his girlfriend. He had no job, no money, and little confidence in their relationship. One of the older men gave him a card for a collection agency that needed phone agents, and then they talked about women. I felt like I was in a locker room, but it was an authentic sharing among strangers.

Riding the bus also keeps me from getting all tangled up in the trauma of commuting, the way I used to. Once, when Alex was a toddler, I was grumbling and cursing someone from behind the wheel when an angelic little voice in the back seat sang out, "Mama, is that a jerk?" I watched my tongue after that.

Old Trophies

Here's Alex with sports trophies we are going to toss. The ski club says no, it can't just glue on new engraved nameplates; they won't take them back. So I took this picture to remember them by. Tomorrow they go into the alley.

Denise

Denise sat awhile on the porch with me tonight. She's
a physician who works very long hours. She's also
very smart and very funny. We met when my *Your Money
or Your Life* study group morphed into a simplicity
group. For three years, about a dozen people met
every two months to reflect on various topics of
simplicity and sustainability. The group dissolved,
but since Denise lives around the corner, we still
get together on my porch or hers.

"What drew you to simplicity, when you don't need
to be frugal?" I asked her.

"When I read about the group, I wasn't even familiar
with the term 'simple living,'" she said. "The way
it was presented was more about living life on your
own terms, and that appealed to me. I'm intrigued
by people who do things their own way. I liked the
diversity of our group and its points of view, and
I liked how the subtext was more about living life
more consciously and meaningfully than getting by
with less."

Then she made one of her brilliant Dr. Denise
observations. "Louis Pasteur said, 'chance favors
the prepared mind,'" she said. "I agree. Only if you
take the time to ponder what you want to do and what
things mean to you, can you make the right kind of
life decisions.

"That's what I like about simplicity: the opportunity
to be authentically myself."

Wine Cellar

Denise is big on wine. She laughed when I told her what my dad said while he was here: "Simple living is not having a wine cellar."

And she disagreed. "If wine is how you enjoy yourself, then simple living is having a wine cellar," she said. "If your summer memories are of sitting on the patio enjoying a really good BLT and a really good French wine, how much better can it get?"

Entertainment

"You probably spend more on entertainment than you do on groceries, clothing, or gasoline," says the *New York Times*. According to the Bureau of Labor Statistics, we spend $200 a month or $2000 a year on cable television, Internet connections, satellite radio, movie tickets and rentals, magazines, live shows, and sporting events.

I checked my records, and the Bureau of Labor Statistics is right. I don't spend anything on cable TV, satellite radio, or sporting events, but there are significant entries under "culture"—theater and opera tickets—and "fun"—everything else: entertaining people, eating out, skiing, Japanese baths, renting movies, and traveling. That's a big one, since my parents and siblings live on the West Coast.

Actually, I spend more on fun than I do on groceries, clothing, dog food, milk, sundries, wine, gardening supplies, laundry soap, light bulbs and other household supplies, clothing, haircuts, cars and gasoline, books, Christmas presents, Alex's school expenses, telephones, exercise, *and* disability and life insurance!

Wow. I'm embarrassed to admit that I checked these numbers to prove I was different than most people. This is not the result I expected.

Doing the math again, it seems that culture and fun expenses roughly equal what I saved in my SEP-IRA and 403B and donated to church, cultural and political causes. Adding in college savings for Alex puts savings-and-gifts about 25 percent ahead of fun and culture.

Am I incredibly indulgent when it comes to culture and fun or incredibly cheap about everything else?

Right here, right now, I'm discovering again the amazing power of tracking expenses. We can say anything we want to about who we are and what we value, but numbers will correct us.

Like the saying goes, show me your checkbook and your calendar, and I'll show you what you value. Turns out I value a good time.

Culture

In *Tuesdays with Morrie*, Morrie Schwartz tells
Mitch Albom not to buy into contemporary mass
culture but to "make your own culture."

Morrie, says Albom, led discussion groups,
square danced, read, wrote letters, "and wasted
no time in front of TV sitcoms or 'Movies of
the Week.'" Instead he "created a cocoon of
human activities—conversation, interaction,
affection."

I'm still embarrassed about my fun-and-culture
expenses—I should be a more serious person,
certainly—but I feel better if I think of them
as an investment in creating my culture.

Japanese baths and opera, trips west, and
having people to dinner. My culture.

Abundance

Speaking of culture, ours defines abundance one way—plenty of food, clothing, stuff, and money to spend—but God defines it another.

I struggle with the concept of abundance. Is it about contentment, about wanting what we already have instead of always wanting more? That's what I believe when I'm sitting on the back porch with

my coffee, face warmed by the sun, taking in the garden. All those experiences are gifts from God, available practically free.

Is it about being able to recognize and accept the gifts of others? That seems plausible when Dottie, who's about 83, stands up and shares a couple of old-fashioned jokes during coffee hour. ("A little boy asks his mother, 'What's that brass plaque on the wall of the church?' 'Oh,' she replies, 'it honors men who were killed in the service.' 'Which service, Mom, the 9 o'clock or the 11?'")

Is it about sharing our abundance with one another, so that all have enough? Maybe.

All I know for sure is that God's abundance is not ours. Abundance is not about my stuff or my bank account. It might be about the amazing blue of Lake Michigan this afternoon, as I rode my bike along the lake, or the scent of the basil in today's box of vegetables.

Where the Lord's Prayer bids, "your kingdom come," a pastor I knew says, "your culture come." I like that. Imagine how well we will understand abundance and how little we will worry when God's culture comes. Meanwhile, a culture sounds easier to create than a kingdom.

Free Lunch

Thinking about abundance, I looked up Isaiah 55, one of my favorite passages:

Ho, everyone who thirsts,
come to the waters;
and you that have no money,
come, buy and eat!
Come, buy wine and milk
without money and without price.
Why do you spend your money for
    that which is not bread,
and your labor for that which
does not satisfy?
Listen carefully to me, and
    eat what is good,
and delight yourselves in rich food.
Incline your ear, and come to me;
listen, so that you may live

(Isaiah 55:1-3).

I love these verses for their evidence of God's generosity. About it, our former pastor Gary once said in a sermon, "See, the universe is a free lunch! We're the ones who decided to charge each other for this handed-over-on-a-platter universe. When we say there is no free lunch, we're agreeing to life with price tags."

Life with price tags. That's pretty much the opposite of abundance. How very sad that we insist on turning most of what God gave us for free into something we can profit from!

Mongo

When the garbage truck came down the alley today, there was a pink teddy bear strapped to its front. I read recently that garbage men call these discarded animals "mongo." It seems the City of New York Department of Sanitation's artist-in-residence (now *there's* an interesting job!) has investigated the phenomenon. Mongo are put on trucks not just for decoration, she says, but also to punish the rescued animals because the garbage collectors feel frustrated with their low-prestige jobs. So she went out and shook hands with every single NYC garbage man and woman, to try and convey a message about the dignity of all work and the benefit we get from garbage collectors!

We don't pay much attention to the people who take away our garbage for us—the official garbage collectors, the men and women with shopping carts who collect discarded cans, and the metal scavengers who pick up old stoves and metal scrap in their dilapidated pickups.

I thought alleys were awfully exotic when I first moved to Chicago. Sacramento only had alleys in the downtown grid. Where A Street, B Street, C Street, and the other lettered streets ended, alleys gave way to a distinctly less urban approach to streets. I was very proud that our street happened to have a tiny little alley, the only one in the neighborhood.

Alleys were so...so *used* in Chicago. At the back of our first apartment was an old door where ice cubes were once delivered. At the base of the building was a coal flue. A few weeks after I moved to Chicago, I swore I heard a ragman going out back shouting for rags. It was 1983; I must have been dreaming!

Pedestrians used alleys for shortcuts. People washed their cars. Kids played. For several summers, the moms on our block would hang out in the evenings while our little boys played baseball and tag.

Alleys have so much life, it's no wonder that the late Monsignor Egan of Chicago said once, "I'd rather have an alley in Chicago than all the boulevards in Paris."

But with life, there's garbage. And we do rely on a host of people to whisk everything away, no matter how greasy, grimy, or dangerous it is. Civic services are a wonderful thing, but I wonder how our way of life has been affected by our ability to let someone else handle our garbage. How would we live if we had to get rid of our trash ourselves?

Garbage

- Garbage production in the U.S. has doubled in the last 30 years.
- 80 percent of U.S. products are used once then thrown away.
- 95 percent of all plastic, 2/3 of all glass containers, and 50 percent of all aluminum beverage cans are never recycled.
- The average American discards 7 pounds of trash per day.
- In Germany, an artist installed 1000 life-sized figures made of discarded computers, tin cans, and other trash in front of the Cologne Cathedral.

Electricity

The summer electric bill is climbing, even though I have no air conditioner. That's a legacy of growing up in central California, where we shut the windows and shutters during the day and opened them at night. Of course, the Central Valley cools off at night; here, it can be sticky all the time. But like Stina Kajsa, I grit my teeth and hold out. When it's really hot, we sleep in the basement.

For two years I've been part of a pilot program that uses Residential Hourly Energy Pricing (RHEP). A special meter records my electrical usage by the hour so that I can be billed exactly the price that Commonwealth Edison pays from hour to hour. People who don't participate in this program pay the average rate.

On hot, muggy days, when electric rates are high, the RHEP people send an e-mail showing the cost of electricity by hour for the next 24. Typically, it's cheaper late at night, so I wait until right before bed to turn on the dishwasher or start a load of wash.

Originally, the RHEP program forecast savings of about 10 percent for its participants. Last year I saved $56.53 or 14.35 percent over the regular rate. Savings in the summer averaged about 13 percent and reached 21.17 percent in December, even though it gets dark earlier and the Christmas lights are on.

This year, electricity is more expensive, and those high-price e-mails arrive daily. I saved 11.4 percent in June, but this month I'm paying about 3 percent *more* than the typical consumer. That's still less than RHEP participants with air conditioners.

I'm sticking with the program, though. I like to think of all the pollutants I'm keeping out of the air by using compact fluorescent light bulbs and forgoing air conditioning. And the RHEP project people say that the results of this pilot are influencing energy policy across the country. Apparently nobody believed that consumers who paid by the hour would change their behavior. But we are!

ComEd is convinced and plans to offer this program to everybody next year.

Total ESPP	Comparable Rate 1 Bill	ESPP Savings	Percentage Savings
$26.47	$33.58	$7.11	21.17%
$26.52	$30.74	$4.22	13.73%
$25.28	$30.61	$5.33	17.41%
$25.96	$31.21	$5.25	16.82%
$30.35	$34.16	$3.81	11.15%
$36.54	$41.85	$5.31	12.69%
$34.92	$40.16	$5.24	13.05%
$29.17	$33.58	$4.41	13.13%
$33.02	$39.18	$6.16	15.72%
$31.26	$36.53	$5.27	14.43%
	$43.33	$4.42	10.44%
	$3.53		14.35%

Electricity consumption per capita per person per year:

U.S.:
13,241 kilowatt hours

The world:
2,361 kilowatt hours

China:
1,139 kilowatt hours

India:
561 kilowatt hours

Heat

With the south-facing windows and transom shut to
keep the really hot air out, it's about 79 degrees
inside my apartment. Ceiling fans make it easier
to sleep, but I wish a big thunderstorm would
rumble through and cool things down. If I open
the front and back doors, the wind races right
down the hallway taking all the heat out.

About air conditioning, I am Amish and stubborn.
There's a little Stina Kajsa here, too, the part
that says: generations of people lived without
this, so I can too.

Water

It's so hot we worshipped
in the church basement
today. Cold bottles of
water were passed out to
everyone. Refreshing and
convenient, yes, but I've
read that Americans spend
$10,000 every minute for
bottled water. Globally,
it's a $46 billion
industry. Funny that we
shun our own tap water
("old-fashioned Chicago
water," I once heard it
described by a waiter who
wanted to sell me mineral
water) that we support
through our taxes. And
then spend more taxes
to dispose of all that
plastic!

Instead of spending
money on bottled water,
we could invest it in
organizations that
provide safe drinking
water in places where
people die of water-
borne illnesses and where
girls can't go to school
because they spend their
days carrying water home
from distant wells.

Redirect the money
from Coca-Cola and Pepsi
to grass-roots water
development projects—
we could call it *water*
democracy.

Cell Phone

More food democracy today in Osseo, Wisconsin, where I had an enormous slab of rhubarb pie at Osseo's famous pie restaurant, the Norski Nook.

My work team stopped there on our way to Fargo, North Dakota, where we'll put on an event. Cell phones helped our eight-person, three-vehicle caravan stay in touch on the road and plan our pie break.

My colleagues must be getting tired of my cell phone message. For two years it's had the same excited message I recorded the day I bought it: "Hi, you've reached Anne and her new cell phone!"

It *was* exciting to buy a cell phone. I put it off for so long, only caving in when my colleagues insisted. We use our phones as walkie-talkies all day long during these summer events, and I was out of the loop.

Except for summer events, I turn out to be a light cell phone user. Alex has never wanted one, probably because he doesn't want his whereabouts tracked. So, no calls from him. My parents and siblings could hardly be less interested. My friends, too, mostly use their landlines for real conversations. And up in the mountains at Holden, cell phones don't work at all.

With half a dozen calls a month, the pay-as-you-go option works best. It's more per minute but lots less per month, and when I want to refill I just dial a couple numbers and it charges my credit card.

It's a real convenience, like my dishwasher, my push lawnmower, and my dryer. Line drying is the best, but when a forgotten tissue sprinkles a load of wash with lint, I'm grateful to be able to run our clothes through the dryer with a fabric softener sheet. Late at night, when the electricity rates are low, of course.

Simple living isn't about spurning convenience; it's more about choosing when and where to make convenience a priority. For me, dishwashers and cell phones are important; outsourcing lawn care or living on take-out food doesn't work for me.

Convenience

More great conveniences:

- automatic paycheck deposits
- automatic tax refund deposits
- my monthly Chicago Transit Authority (CTA) pass, automatically reloaded by my employer
- checking the CTA pass balance online
- automatic mortgage payment withdrawal
- home-delivered milk
- home-delivered vegetables
- heat, hot water, cooking gas, electricity!
- my vintage Electrolux vacuum
- three different I-Go cars parked three blocks away

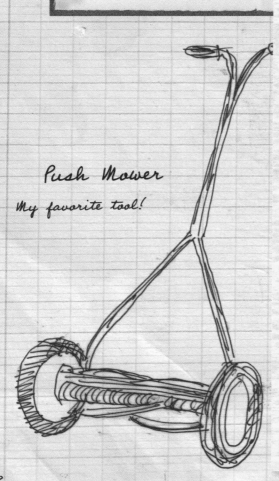

Push Mower

My favorite tool!

Anniversary

Today is—or would be—my 20th wedding anniversary.
I got to wondering: how many of my simple choices would
I have made if I had been married all these years?
Divorced, most of my decisions have been my own. I never
had to convince a spouse, compromise, or set aside
desires altogether for the good of the relationship.

That's the upside, along with having plenty of time for
friends and community activities. The downside has been
spending most of Alex's life cut off from the one other
person who loves him as I do. Rarely have we compared
notes or shared joys or concerns. Alex's dad has been
a silent partner in Alex's upbringing—always there,
but inaccessible to me. That part has been very lonely.

It's funny to me that, to maintain continuity for Alex,
I've stuck to some of the decisions about life we made
years ago—like staying in the house we bought together,
instead of subjecting Alex to the additional upheaval
of moving or leaving Chicago; staying in the same
congregation; remaining part of his dad's family, even
when his dad is estranged.

More than autonomy, it has been good health that let
me embrace simplicity and shape a good life. I have the
luxury of making choices because I'm healthy. If I've
cut back or pared down, it has been to make more space
for good things in our life, not to try to keep pace
with escalating medical bills.

Replace this bedrock stability with illness or tragedy,
and things would be difficult. Life would have been
different if Alex were medically fragile or had any
special needs. A suspicious mammogram could change
everything tomorrow.

Rain

On my bank's message boards is one of those signs urging passersby to set aside something for a rainy day. The problem is, some rainy days—like poor health and catastrophe—just go on and on and no amount of money in the bank can really help.

Holden

Alex is on his way to visit my brother John in Washington State. Next week the two of them will hike across the Cascades to Holden Village.

Having been dragged from one community meeting to another for most of his childhood, Alex was suspicious the first time we went to Holden. By the end of our week, he was sold.

How could he resist a tiny, remote mountain village where there are no phones and no television, but there is a perfect blend of learning, conversation, hiking, eating, worship, and fun? Where each of us could weave a complex, independent social life and still share the same room? Right away he fell in love with the pool hall. That's where he was assigned to work the next year, when we returned as volunteers, and that's been his job ever since. Next year he hopes to run the pool hall for the whole summer.

Me, I'm a housekeeper and, as needed, a painter, a gardener, a musician, a worship leader, a teacher. Holden has been good to me. The '90s were difficult: two divorces, all that financial instability, a biopsy for breast cancer (negative, thankfully), much wrangling with my ex over Alex's upbringing. Moments of joy and contentment always outweighed the tough times (mostly because I was working at home; could I have managed all those traumas *and* worked fulltime in an office?), but I was glad when that decade ended.

The year when Alex and I first visited Holden was the year that my life perked up. Surely there is a relationship; surely the new vistas and new people it brought into our lives opened possibilities for both of us. Six visits later, we are regulars; our weeks there are the highlight of our year.

People get hooked on Holden, but not my parents. "Your dad never really *got* Holden," my mom said about our visits there when I was a child. I got enough to know how to get back, 30 years later, and pass the gift of Holden on to Alex. Now he can always find his way back to another place in the world where he's anchored.

Offering

Putting my envelope in the offering today, I thought: this is sacramental, letting go of "my" money, sending it to the altar. When I pay bills or donate to a cause, I write the check, address the envelope, stick on a stamp, and mail it to a recipient I've chosen. Every step in the process is mine to guide. But making an annual commitment and following through slightly shifts the balance of power. My power ends when I set the envelope in the plate.

Roommates

My friend and former tenant Ann stayed over tonight. It's so quiet without Alex, I was grateful for the company.

For years, I had lots of company. After Max moved out, his sister Carol moved in. Her marriage was also foundering, and she needed someplace to stay.

When she found a new place, my brother John moved in. He had just been discharged from the Navy Reserve and wanted to see the world.

Living with him was easy, because as siblings we did most things practically the same way. He was a very mellow presence with a very big appetite. I had to cook plenty because he'd always push back from the table and say, "time for thirds." He was kind to Alex, although Alex was not kind to him. When Alex was grumpy, he would growl, "I hate you," to John. Poor guy, with no friends in a big city and no job for some time too, having to endure that abuse. But it gave their relationship a significant foundation, because today John is Alex's favorite uncle. We were sad when he moved back west two years later.

For three years, Carol and John amplified our little household. There was more company at the table—a greater sense of family for Alex at mealtimes—and the extra rental income was welcome. John helped out around the house, especially with painting outside trim.

When my dad was a boy, so many visiting preachers lodged with his family that the basement bedroom was known as "the prophet's chamber." I think of my basement bedroom as "the transition room" because it's been a refuge for Carol, John, and a couple other folks who were struggling from one part of life to another. And most truly settled people are not very interested in living in someone else's basement.

These days my visitors are short-term folks who are just passing through. Like Ann, who stays every couple of months when she needs to be in Chicago. Instead of a strategy for subsidizing my housing costs and filling seats at the table, it's become a ministry of hospitality. Sometimes I think welcoming the stranger is the most critical work there is, and I'm glad to be able to use my extra room to do it.

Thirds

"Time for thirds," John used to say.

Simplicity isn't drudgery, dullness, or some kind of dingy, Soviet plan that forces us to redistribute what is "rightfully ours."

It's really just about passing up thirds.

Most Americans had firsts a century ago. We started getting seconds a couple decades ago. Now it seems to me that we stuff ourselves all the time.

Seagull

Another image of greed from a walk on the beach: a seagull, guarding a pile of bread crumbs, so vigilant about keeping the other seagulls away that he had no time to actually eat any crumbs. He couldn't lean over and nibble for fear that another bird would steal some! From my perspective, making a feast for everyone looked like a better option.

Salad

Red leaf lettuce, green leaf lettuce, mesclun, spinach—
the first few vegetable deliveries are all greens. It's
overwhelming—and tiring! I have to have salad with
everything in order to keep up.

In the summer, I don't go to the store much. Vegetables
arrive every Saturday, and milk gets delivered every
Friday, year round. I still make those monthly runs to the
discount store for flour, noodles, and rice, but
everything else comes to me. That's a plus, for someone
without a car. All I need to do is pick up some chicken
breasts and a bottle of wine from the store every couple
of weeks.

Sue

Every Saturday night at
10:00 p.m., I check the
back porch to see whether
all the CSA vegetable
boxes have been picked
up. Usually at least one
box is left over; there
might be three or four. I
load two boxes at a time
into my shopping cart and
haul them around the
corner to my neighbor
Sue's house.

Sue is a visiting nurse
whose clients live in a
particularly notorious
Chicago housing project.
She visits them very
early, from 5:00 to 7:00
a.m., always with a
security guard. "That's
when the guys with guns
are asleep," she says.

Sue repacks the extra
vegetables into five
or six bags and leaves
them with her homebound
clients. They love
getting them! For years,
there was no close source
of fresh produce. The
only stores willing to
operate there were tiny,
cramped, security-barred
places that carried
potato chips and bourbon
but not broccoli.

Today there's a big
new supermarket nearby,
but her clients don't
get out much, and they
still appreciate the
home delivery. She says
that every May they
start asking, "When are
the vegetables coming?"

My furniture, from the alley:
- The orange and green rug in the hallway (washed)
- The rag rug on the back porch (washed)
- A tin candle stand, like a Mexican luminaria (good as is)
- A small end table (painted; it's now my TV stand)
- A rocking armchair (re-upholstered)
- A curly maple, glass-fronted bookcase, glass broken (sold for $100 at a garage sale!)

Milk Bottles

The *clink* of glass bottles is one of the earliest
sounds I remember—that and hearing my parents play
the piano. So when home delivery milk came back to
Chicago, I wanted Alex to know that sound. I wanted
him to heft gallon jugs from the porch and walk
them to the fridge. I wanted to use less plastic,
and growth hormones made me nervous.

The milk comes every Friday. It's more expensive
than milk from the store. It's way more expensive
than the powdered milk that tightwads swear by.
Every glass is worth it, especially with a warm
cookie or a plate of tuna casserole.

And now I know it's food democracy, too!

Tomorrow I leave for Holden, speaking of frugality
and powdered milk. Time to cancel the milk. Too
bad—I'll miss it.

Lodge

I have my own single room this year. Five years
of rooming with Alex have drawn to a close.
He's rooming with his friend Micah.

Living out of a suitcase in a single room is
downright restful. Laundry and grooming are my
only personal responsibilities. I brush my
teeth, wash my face, and am ready for the day.
My commute to work is 90 seconds—counting a
stop for coffee—instead of an hour and 15
minutes. When my housekeeping shift is done,
there's all the time in the world to enjoy a
walk, a meal, a hike, a conversation, or a nap
on a porch swing.

Here, I am at my slowest. That's not saying
much, really; my slow is other people's fast.
But now and then I can feel a different rhythm
emerging in my bones. Yesterday Alex and I took
a long, steep hike on our day off. Then I
soaked in the hot tub (outdoors, with a view of
the trail we had just taken up the mountain),
plunged into the cold stream, and went to the
snack bar for ice cream. Walking back to my
room, I noticed how relaxed I felt, how
dreamily I was moving: Oh! I thought. This must
be what it's like to slow down.

Grateful

Surrounded by beauty, it's easy to feel grateful
for God's gifts, from the first rays of sun on
the mountains until the stars blaze in the sky.
Chicago is on the same earth and under the same
stars, but stars are obscured by buildings,
traffic, congestion. In my urban environment,
it's harder to feel grateful. I don't wake up and
thank God for the sidewalk, the curb, the garbage
cans, the bus driver, my fellow passengers, my
colleagues. But it's all from God.

Potty Patrol

Today I straightened up
Potty Patrol, a wall of
shelves lined with lost
items that people have
never claimed (often left
in the lodge bathrooms;
hence the name) or stuff
they donated on purpose.
It's an endless source
of clothing and personal
care supplies. My friend
John brags that he only
spends $10 a year on
personal care items
because he can stock up
here all summer long.
Me, too! Today I picked
up a half-used bottle of
chamomile shampoo and a
tube of hand lotion. I'm
keeping my eye out for
more. I like keeping the
plastic out of Holden's
waste stream and lowering
my pharmacy bill, too.

Organizing the shelves
also lets me get a good
look at the clothing
inventory. So far this
year I've found a nice
summer shift, a lilac
Polar fleece pullover,
and a red Polar fleece
vest. The lilac pullover
is in perfect condition
but the red vest has a
little paint on it.

The other day I chose a
pair of sneakers to wear
when I swim in the creek.
The day we leave, I'll
put them back on the
Potty Patrol shelf for
someone else.

I've often wished that
there were something like
this out in the real
world—a sort of giant
returns department where
you could swap purchases
you regretted or had
outgrown for something
more useful.

Shredding

There's a new task for Holden housekeepers this year: shredding.

Shredders have certainly gone from accessory to necessity in record time. Identity theft is such a frightening possibility, it's no wonder we're willing to shred anything with an account number, a social security number, or an address.

Privacy is important. I guess that's why after a morning of vacuuming and cleaning bathrooms we now gather on the dock to feed papers through a shredder for half an hour or so. With two people, it's a shredding party—a mindless activity you can talk around.

I usually shred my old checks and financial statements at work, or have a little shredding party with my neighbor Val. She watches TV; I shred. She enjoys the company; I postpone buying a shredder. A few weeks ago I saw my first-ever episode of "Sex and the City." While I shredded, she filled me in on all the details about the characters and their stories. They don't seem to buy their clothes at resale stores.

Tired feet at
Holden Pass

Poetry

Every afternoon I rush from housekeeping to the 3:00 p.m. poetry workshop, taught by Jim from Yakima, Washington. "Write a page a day," he advises. As he folds a sheet of paper in half, then in quarters, then once again, he continues: "Of course, you can decide how big that page will be."

A page a day of poetry is a real challenge, even though I write more than a page a day for a living. I've put it aside for the last few years, but this workshop is so stimulating, maybe I should get back to it.

Flow

We are awake and conscious about 16 hours each day. In a week we spend:

- 24 to 60 hours on productive activities like working or just being at work (where we don't always work), or, for young people, studying.

- 20 to 42 hours on maintenance activities like housework, eating, grooming ourselves, and transportation.

- 20 to 43 hours on leisure activities like reading or watching TV, playing sports or eating out, talking, or idling and resting.

That's according to Mihaly Csikszentmihalyi, author of *Finding Flow: The Psychology of Engagement in Everyday Life*, which I borrowed from the Holden library.

Life at Holden is organized so that for guests, anyway, almost no time has to be spent on maintenance activities. Everyone eats together, so individuals don't have to shop and cook. Children's programs give parents a few hours of freedom to engage in discussions and crafts. Tiny lodge rooms limit the possessions we need to take care of. Nobody has to drive. There's maximum time for reading, talking, and learning— the good stuff, as far as I'm concerned.

How many of us take this lesson home—that if we owned less and did more collectively, we could all shift more time from maintenance to leisure?

What's freeing about this list for me is the notion that some tasks just come with being human, and I can just stop fretting. I don't like ironing, but it will never go away.

Do Not Be Conformed

Living at Holden makes me remember the church
bulletin with Romans 12 on it that I used to keep
tucked into my bedroom mirror, for courage. "Do not
conform, but be transformed" kept me brave, able to
press ahead with life changes that transformed me.

I love this invitation. It's my mantra.

Do not conform, but be transformed.
Yes, I can resist consumer culture!

Do not conform, but be transformed.
Yes, I can talk to Alex or sit on the porch instead
of watching TV.

Do not conform, but be transformed.
Yes, I can sell my car and live without one.

Do not conform, but be transformed.
Yes, I can work at home and be there for Alex.

Do not conform, but be transformed.
Yes, hand-me-down clothes are a gift!

Do not conform, but be transformed.
Yes, I can appreciate what I have instead of always
wanting more.

Do not conform, but be transformed.
Yes, I can borrow CDs from the library instead of
buying them.

Do not conform, but be transformed.
Yes, it's okay to shop at garage sales.

Do not conform, but be transformed.
Yes, I can say no once in awhile and rest.

Do not conform, but be transformed.
Yes, God is inviting me to deepen my understanding
of God's culture and to try to live God's principles
in my faltering, imperfect way.

Out

"Going out"—that is, leaving Holden—is hard.
The first difference is garbage. Because
throwing things away in the wilderness means
carting it down the mountain to a barge, at
Holden everything is sorted into recycling,
landfill, burnable, or compost. Paper is sorted
into four different categories. What a shock,
after such careful stewardship, to be asked to
throw everything into the same garbage can! And
then downtown Seattle: a sea of people sporting
t-shirts with brand names or destinations, all
of them shopping. What an orgy of consumption
it seemed, after three weeks away.

The upside to this painful re-entry process
is that for a few days, anyway, I can "see"
our culture more objectively than usual. I can
notice our patterns of life, reflect on the
decisions that led us to create them, and
imagine what kind of decisions might create
patterns that are more wholesome for us and
our planet.

Home Again

Mihaly Csikszentmihalyi, where are you?

After three weeks living in a small dorm room, my home is a giant to-do list. It needs cleaning, vacuuming, shopping, grass cutting, weeding, sweeping, and on and on and on.

Maintenance, maintenance, maintenance.

Cleaning usually brings me joy. Gardening will be a treat, once I've caught up on everything the house sitter neglected. (I did find one. She wasn't very good.) But today the contrast is stark between my fully equipped normal life and the stripped-down version I left at Holden.

Without Alex, 1100 square feet feel enormous. I could move. I'd spend less time maintaining things in an apartment with no yard, tenants, or basement. But I'd never talk over the back fence with my neighbors. No one would ring my doorbell. I couldn't sit on the front porch and watch the world go by, or chat with folks while I'm pushing the lawnmower. I'd have fewer extra beds and could welcome fewer guests. I'd have more time for me, but less connection to my surroundings.
Selling and moving runs against my family's grain. We hang on to houses for decades. My grandfather built the house I grew up in. My mother still owns the

one he bought before that, in 1919! Our family farm was purchased in 1890. My house is 100 years old this year and, for about 20 percent of that century, I've been its owner.
Packing up and leaving won't be easy. I don't want to do it until I know more about what's happening next. I've been an empty nester all of 10 days. No need to rush!

Dorm Room

I visited Alex in his new dorm room. A note on the whiteboard over his bed said, "My mom is coming today."

We looked at photos of his hike to Holden, and he showed me around the floor. So far, he's very excited to have a dorm room, a roommate, new friends, a class schedule. It looks like college, smells like college, tastes like college, so it must be college. I'll try to relax.

Work

All-day meetings are
so tiring. After my
colleague Kevin
dropped me off
tonight, I cooked some
taco casserole, walked
Barks twice, and laid
down. Lights were off at
9:45 p.m. Of course, Spanish
started again today, so it was the
first time since July that I had
to get going at 5:30 a.m. A long,
long day.

Set out in the alley:
The big brown armchair
from the front room. Five
years ago we dragged it in
from the alley after my
next door neighbor set it
out. I'm tired of it. Back
it goes.

Stress

Work is still hard. I get stressed handling multiple demands. Sometimes I'm so overwhelmed by the expectations that I freeze. There are so many possible tasks to tackle, I don't know what to do next!

Working at home was never like this. I only handled a few projects at a time, and all my clients were safely at the other end of a phone line. They didn't stop by to see how things were going or change the assignment. But in an office my priorities shift with every encounter. It's dizzying.

A really bad day at the office is draining, soul killing. A really bad day at home has more escape valves: time out for a walk, a few minutes with a book, in extreme emergencies, a hot bath. At the office, I can always take a stroll through the corporate forest, but I keep forgetting to. The office is so insular, so absorbing. To leave it I have to go down ten floors and push through revolving doors, and then I'm in a driveway.

I'm becoming more like my dog Barks, who looks like a puppy, but is 11 years old. In the first delirious moments of a walk, he bounds down the alley, tail wagging. He keeps his pace up pretty well, but when he gets home he collapses on the floor and rests for a really long time.

Me, too. I start the day bursting with energy and end it whacked. I'm getting old, too.

Enough

Balancing the checkbook, I realized I forgot to enter one whole August paycheck. No wonder I've been short on money lately!

Discovering the error made me laugh. To think that I would forget to enter a paycheck when all through the lean '90s I spent at least two evenings a month at my desk worrying about money. I would forecast what I was likely to pull in from my freelance business and then look at the bills. Some months I could cover everything beautifully. Other months took juggling.

This ritual made anguish as familiar a flavor as the chocolate chip cookies Alex and I baked. Simplifying expenses plus getting regular paychecks has banished the taste—well, not so much *banished* as *replaced* it with a new flavor: sure, I have enough now, but will there *always* be "enough"?

My mom says this question preoccupies my father.

"Some days he looks at what we have and thinks it's plenty," she says. "Other days he looks at the same amount and is certain we will run out of money in our old age." How much they have doesn't change; only how he feels about it.

I'm not even 50, and this is my question, too! It engages all of us. Will there be enough if we live to 90? Will we have to work forever? Can we count on social security, pensions, or any kind of support? Will our children help or even remember us if they live in another city?

Worrying about enough for the long run leaches the pleasure out of right now. And I wonder whether our quest to have more things is a strange way of reassuring ourselves that the answer is yes.

Once I visited a family that had every toy and tool ever made. In the garage were a car for each grownup and bikes, skis, stuff to take to the beach, kites, volleyball nets, a kayak.

Crammed metal shelves lined the walls.

The overstuffed look continued in the kitchen: hundreds of cookbooks, 24 kinds of tea, appliances on every counter.

In the basement guest room where I stayed, the bookshelves were teeming. They looked a little neglected, like the exercise room next door.

This family loved their home and their stuff, their suburban hillside and forest view. The parents might have loved it more than they loved each other, because big cracks in the marriage were apparent. It made me uneasy. It was too much— more than they could ever need, use, or enjoy. And even it wouldn't always be enough!

Years ago a good friend was mugged by a man who pushed her down, grabbed her purse, and ran off with her money, credit cards, and keys. Several months later the police called to say they had found her purse in a pile of purses in an empty apartment. That pile always gave me pause. Was it a sort of savings account for the thief— something he watched grow with pride? Did it somehow reassure him that yes, through his particular talent, there was and would always be enough?

Walking Home

Tonight I got off the bus at Clark Street, the main street for my neighborhood. In every storefront was something worth admiring: toys at the Swedish museum, new titles at the bookstore, the shiny V-8 engine at the auto parts store. Lots of folks on foot, too. There are plenty of cars and buses, but on this stretch, pedestrians rule. There's just the right amount of clutter and noise. Strolling home, enjoying the familiar, I felt welcomed, like I belonged here.

Perfect Saturday

Today was a pleasure, from start to finish:

- I woke without the alarm, a little later than usual, with no sense of having to rush off.
- Made coffee and sipped it in the back yard, watching orange butterflies alighting on the purple buddleia bushes. White autumn clematis has spread all along the fence, over the buddleia, and up my neighbor Tom's birch tree.
- Made a bouquet for the kitchen. Purple, red, a splash of orange, set off nicely by a blue vase and blue-checked tablecloth.
- Did errands on my bike, on streets I haven't ridden lately.
- Visited with my friend who's here from Boston. We ate carrot soup and took a walk around the park.
- Ate lunch with Dick.
- Vacuumed, cleaned, and scrubbed the house while listening to *Manon Lescaut* on the radio.
- Cut the grass and dug up and seeded the bare spots. I was focused on the horizon under my knees: weeds, worms, dirt, dead grass. But at one point I looked up at the profusion of plants hanging from Tom's porch. So many colors and textures, and I never look up and notice!
- Washed the basement rug at the laundromat.
- And at the end of this vigorous day, I took a bath.

What a perfect balance of people and solitude, of labor and rest. The house and the garden look nice. I will sleep well.

Sunday

Today's New Testament lesson, from Paul: "If I am to live in the flesh, that means fruitful labor for me."

That was me, yesterday!

Laundry

Alex called.

"I know it's a cliché, Mom, but can I come
home and do my laundry?"

While his clothes were in the washer and dryer
(no time for line drying today!), he baked a
batch of chocolate chip cookies and took half of
them back to pass out in his dorm.

I found two shredders
in the alley—one on a
dumpster, one inside
it. The one I brought
home works just fine.

Vegetables

When I signed up to host the vegetable site, I was
a freelancer who stuck close to home. Now I've got
a job that takes me out of town at least three
weeks a summer. Adding in Holden, I'm gone six
weeks. That's a lot of Saturday vegetables to ask
someone else to handle.

I'm thinking about resigning as host at the end of
this season. On the plus side, I won't have to be
home part of every Saturday or arrange a substitute
to open and close the site and get the extras to
Sue. On the down side, the vegetables will cost
twice as much, because I'll lose my 50 percent
discount. Also, I'll have to go somewhere else to
get my box. That was easy five years ago, when I
still owned a car. It will be harder now.

But I think I'm going to do this, anyway.

Tomatoes

Yum, my favorite lunch:
a homemade bacon,
lettuce, and tomato
sandwich with farm
tomatoes and lettuce.

Fresh BLTs are so good,
I refuse to order them
from restaurants or make
them at any other time of
year. I just can't face a
pink tomato when I know
the alternative—huge
hybrids and heirloom
varieties with yellow and
red stripes, red and
green stripes, and all
shades of red. They are
big and ripe and juicy,
and paired with a little
fresh butter lettuce,
mayonnaise, hot bacon,
and a glass of milk,
there's no better lunch.

I never get tomato
fatigue. Bring on the
tomatoes, farm! Besides

BLTs, there's my favorite
fresh tomato sauce—
tomatoes, bacon, garlic,
a little red pepper, and
heaps of fresh basil, all
sautéed and served over
hot noodles. I can also
freeze sauce and even
whole tomatoes. I learned
that from my colleague

Ruth, who gave me two
bagsful last fall. It was
so funny, to see plum
tomatoes frozen hard!
They'd be deadly if they
were thrown, but they
melt into sauce as soon
as they are warmed.

Community Garden

Four days in New York for work. I spent Saturday with
my friend Jan in her community garden in Brooklyn.
This beautiful corner, just teeming with plants and
people and energy, has nurtured her through all her
years in a great big city.

"Do you ever get tired of sharing?" I asked.

"Sure," she said. "It can be really difficult at times.
Sometimes we have knock-down, drag-out fights over how
to use the land. Some people who volunteer are really
needy. When I coordinated the volunteers for our last
workday, I swear I was mom to everybody. Anything and
everything they needed, they came to me.

"Sometimes I wish I had my own garden, but that's
impossible here unless you own a house. It's community
that makes the garden possible, so in the end, it's
worth it."

Alice

In the garden I talked to Alice, an artist who lives with her husband in a coop loft in Brooklyn.

"I'm a pack rat with a large apartment," she told me. "I like lending things to others. Some of my items are on permanent loan.

"I have a canning kettle I found under a tree 12 years ago. When I'm not cooking jam, I lend it to people for cooking, canning, and dying.

"I lend extra blankets when my neighbors have guests.

"I lend out my fish poacher—a wonderful thing to share because you use it so rarely.

"I lend trays, platters, and other party stuff, especially CorningWare. I label it with those address labels you get free in the mail.

"I have a really nice collection of aprons that I lend to bake sales. When kids use them, the pockets make them feel so grownup.

"I keep odds and ends of serving platters and cookware to send leftovers home. I call them my "alien dishes" because sometimes I get different ones back!

"Before we give a party, we take our knives over to a friend's house and use his electric knife sharpener. He would let us take it home but we feel more comfortable using it there.

"I lend my 10-quart stock pot to Sally to make Latino rice pudding. How often do you need a 10-quart pot?

"We always keep a stack of chairs in the hall outside our apartment for people to borrow for parties.

"I also lend my toilet plunger. Really, I do! Ours are the really sturdy old-fashioned kind that can unplug anything. Not like those flimsy ones most people have nowadays."

Totems

Today I passed a woman holding
three powerful totems of urban life:
a Starbucks cup, a Blockbuster DVD,
and a plastic bag of dry cleaning.
I imagined her life: Fuel for the
journey. A movie for a solo evening
at home. And a wardrobe of expensive,
fragile clothes that she can't wash
herself.

Fall

www.elca.org/hunger/resources/simple/sustaining.html

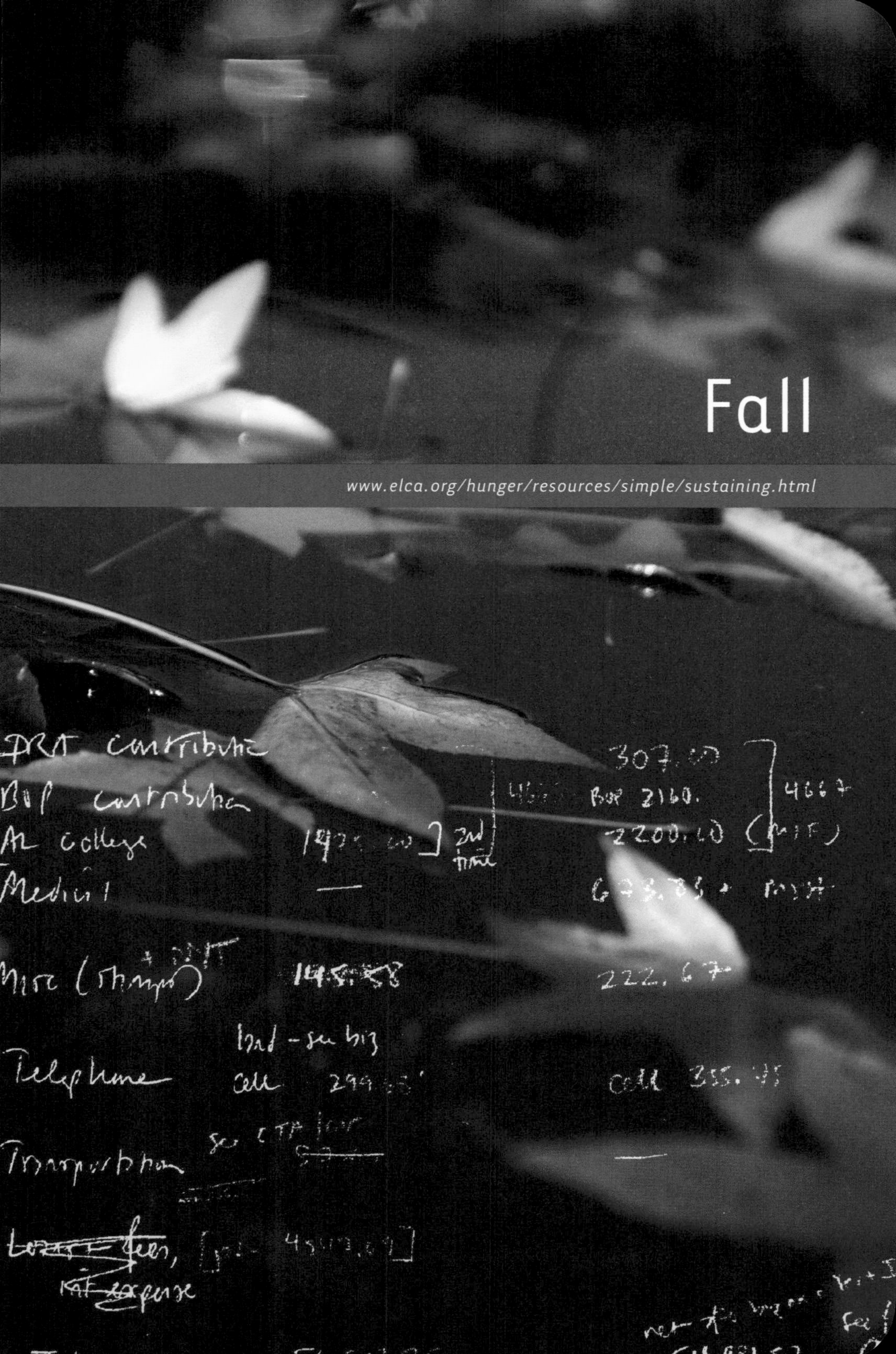

Dick in his
messy kitchen

Farewell Convertible

Kevin is giving away his convertible. Counting
gas, insurance, registration, and the mounting
repairs, he's spending 40 cents a mile to
drive. ("And I drove 18,000 miles last year!
That's $7200!") If his brother and sister-in-
law are willing to fix the transmission,
he's going to give it to them, for their son.

I'll miss the many times we've ridden to and
from work with the top down, with me wearing
my Jackie Onassis scarf and shades! And
all the times I've borrowed it for work and
personal errands. (It's a fleet car, really,
because everybody on our work team has used
it for something.) I've bought him many
tanks of gas and even replaced his windshield
wipers, in gratitude.

He's doing this cold turkey. It will be
interesting to watch!

Mess

Dick turns 91 soon. All of a sudden he is aging quickly. When we meet for lunch, he repeats himself often and can't remember things long enough to act on them. Also, his hearing has degenerated so much that there's no point calling him. His standard funny phone greeting is, "Is that you?" Of course, it's always "you," but he can no longer figure out *which* "you" is speaking. Lately I confirm all of our appointments in person. I've been stopping by a couple times a week, just to make sure he's fine.

His kitchen—in the basement, because his mother didn't want her five children tracking mud upstairs in the front room—is messier and messier. There are papers everywhere: on the table, on chairs, on the kitchen counters, on the cutting board, even on the floor. When Dick looks for something he grins, waves his hands across the tabletop, and says, "It's here! Right here!"

It's about time for him to consider moving into a senior apartment or asking someone to move in with him. It's a quandary, how to encourage a stubborn and independent man that it's time to consider a change. "I'm not getting any younger," he says, "but I'm not ready to move yet."

Today after lunch we went back to his kitchen so he could look for a particular photo of himself taken about 30 years ago. As he sifted through papers, I asked if I could toss out some of the garbage. Sure, he said.

Two hours later, we were still at it. He was a little anxious until I showed him what I was tossing and where I was putting his bills. He found the photo, and uncovered some interesting items from his stacks of clippings, all underlined in red ink. Many of them are related to his interest in what sustains people and why some people live longer and more successfully than others.

"Listen to this," he said. "Rich, educated people commit suicide more often than people who are poor and less educated. It's because poor people know they can't control life, but rich people think they can and when things go wrong, they are more likely to end it."

The garbage pile grew as we talked. Eventually I tossed six big bags and got all the papers off the floor, desk, and kitchen counter. (I wish I could have recycled them.) Then we sifted through the bills, and paid the overdue ones. "I had no idea I had let things get to that state," he kept saying.

Sorting and tossing took me back to my grandfather's three moves. When we moved into his big house, he moved to an apartment. I was too young to help then, but I was part of the next two moves—first, to an apartment building next to our church's senior home, and then into a senior building. Both jobs taxed my mother so much, she went right to work organizing her own house. She swore she and my dad wouldn't leave us a mess when they moved or died.

It isn't that Dick has so much stuff. It's that he is losing his ability to manage paper. He's swamped in fundraising appeals, utility bills, bank deposit slips, Christmas cards, clippings, and old photos.

Paper inundates us and can trip us up. It looks like Dick forgot to pay his homeowner policy, and it has been canceled. If he forgets to pay his real estate taxes, someone could buy his house right out from under him at a tax sale.

It makes me pretty sad.

Stuff

We accumulate things and bring them meaning
and, when we die, their meaning vanishes
with us.

Hard as it is to see perfectly good merchandise
in the alley, it's harder to run across
personal memorabilia. I once found a stack of
old sepia photos next to a dumpster. Forgotten
by the building's previous owner and discarded
by the new one, I suppose. And no one remembered
the men and women in the photos.

When Alex and I helped our neighbor Mildred
clear out her deceased friend Lucille's
apartment, it was the same. Without a family,
there was nothing to do but give away what we
could and toss the rest. Mildred gave me
Lucille's beautiful cobalt blue fruit bowl.
It's a bowl, not an heirloom; I don't know its
story. Neither does Alex. The next person who
owns it won't even know Lucille's name.

We forget this, in the throes of feathering our
nests. If we remembered it, would we acquire a
little less greedily?

Joanne

Joanne was leaving Dick's house as I arrived, pushing herself with a walker. What a shock!

Joanne and her husband Frank were my heroes when I young. They were creative, intellectual, engaged in the life of the community, and their home was smart. What wasn't a family heirloom was something Joanne picked up in a resale shop. She's a genius at second-hand shopping. In a pile of junk, she could find sterling silver.

For years Joanne and I helped sort and price items for our block club's garage sale, because then we could reserve purchases early. Once, in a corner, in a crumpled paper bag, I found a set of Quimper cups and saucers from France. It was exactly the kind of thing Joanne would uncover—and I knew they were valuable. Looking around guiltily, I asked the woman in charge of that section, "Are you saving these for Joanne Williams?" No, she said, and charged me $5.

Frank's Parkinson's kept Joanne home for many years, and her health has declined since he died. Now, she told me, she's trying to dismantle her beautiful house. She has a buyer, but before she can sell and move closer to her son, she needs to find new homes for all those significant objects. The old hand-operated presses have gone to a museum. An antique doll collection has been crated for a niece.
Her son can have the art. But thousands of books need to be sifted into keep and toss piles, and her limited mobility makes it tough. "I can bend over, but I can't be sure that I'll be able to get up again," she chuckled, so she's waiting for her son to show up and help her finish the job.

Suddenly my dearest neighbors, people I have looked up to for years, are frail. If I quit my job tomorrow I could fill my time helping folks like Dick and Joanne pack up their lives for their last journey. It makes me very sad. With no children to push or help, Dick clings stubbornly to his way of life. Joanne is moving on. Both have collections to curate—museums, in a way. Joanne is actively curating her collection. Dick isn't. The family photos stacked on the chair next to the kitchen table will be the first to burn the day he forgets a pan on the stove.

My parents have a museum, too. There are books in Swedish, china and crystal from several generations, a wooden fruit bowl from a great-great-great-great Basye relative, and of course those scowling portraits of Stina Kajsa and Jonas. For now, everything is in its place and, like Dick, there is no thought of change.

We spend so much of life accumulating and tending our stuff and then, old age comes and turns it into a hassle.

"Getting and spending, we lay waste our powers," Wordsworth said in a sonnet. I agree!

Two Rooms

A lovely couple, about the same age as my dad, retired to Florida for many years and then came back to Chicago to be near family. Whatever their museum was, they've relinquished it and are free now; everything they own is in their two-room suite at a beautiful retirement home. They still drive to see their grandchildren and they still go to Florida for the winter, but now they can close the door behind them and not worry at all. "It's like living in a nice hotel with full dining three times a day," she says. They're thrilled.

Museum

Alex's dad is moving again. "This weekend I'm going through my room there and either packing stuff or throwing it away," Alex said.

Alex has some treasured items from his childhood. His stuffed baby Lambchop and a collection of Little Golden books, at my house; Raccoony, another plush, stuffed animal, is at his dad's, I think.

"If there's anything you want to keep that Dad doesn't have room for, you can store it here," I said, thus opening my own museum.

Empty Nest

"When my daughter was a child, I felt like I was CEO of the world's most exciting company," says my colleague Kate. "Then she went to college, and overnight I was out of a job."

Now I know what she means. Alex seems so self-sufficient. Although he's in Chicago, he has his own place to live. They feed him there. His dealings with his teachers are his business, not mine. Even his laundry is his responsibility.

As one-half of a joint parenting agreement, I've had lots of empty-nest practice. Plenty of nights Alex has been at his dad's house, and I've been alone. But I was always looking forward to his return. Now I'm not sure what to look forward to.

My life is full and empty at the same time. Work makes my life much more full than it was eight years ago, but Alex's absence makes it empty. I come home and nobody is there but the dog. I cook, and it's for nobody but me. I don't feel like cleaning. Nobody is coming over. Also, vacuuming is Alex's job. So is baking cookies. Surely I will break down and clean, but will I bake my own cookies?

1983

I have *never* lived alone at this address. Since 1983 there has been more than one name on the mailbox.

I don't feel like cooking *or* cleaning. There are huge dust bunnies under the chairs. The dining room table is piled with my books and papers. When I get home I heat up frozen soup or make an omelet. The other night I ate tortilla chips and herring, because that's what was in the refrigerator.

Was Alex the only reason I ever cleaned or cooked? Have my good housekeeping habits been all about other people? Am I really never going to bother to cook cozy, well-balanced meals for myself? Alex was a big reason I committed to living more simply. It was for him I worked at home, engaged in the community, saved money. Shaping a life I could sustain without having to work all day, every day in an office gave me the freedom to be a better mother.

I need a different freedom now.

FREEdom

Next

Okay, I have an idea for that new freedom.

Alex is in college; I'll go to college, too.

The Holden poetry workshop got me thinking about grad school. On and off, I've written poetry and been part of workshops and literary journals. A few years back I almost applied for a creative writing program, but the time wasn't right. I was still too busy with Alex. Now, though, I have no excuse. I'll apply for January.

I can pay for it with current income, some savings, and, well, equity. How ironic that during those lean, post-divorce years, we lived inside our safety net—an asset whose value increased as our neighborhood got trendier.

Three times I've pulled out money from the building: the first time to buy out Max after our divorce; the second time to upgrade the bathroom and fix financial problems after divorce number two; the third time to tear off and replace the roof. Very Stina, to spend it so carefully. Very Lydia, to imagine a new way to benefit from this resource.

So I can arrange the money for grad school. Arranging the time will be harder. Those years of clear space I carved out in Alex's childhood have filled up.

Schedule

How will I squeeze grad school into a schedule that looks like this?

Four days of work in the office, one day of work at home.

Spanish at 6:45 a.m. Monday and Wednesday, before work.

Wednesday, choir practice. The director is gone this week so I'm leading the rehearsal.

Thursday, my first play with Alex (since he's staying in Chicago, I bought a subscription to the Goodman so we could connect now and then)

Pilates on Friday morning before work.

Saturday I do have some free time, though I have to take care of the vegetables. Ski season is coming, and then every Saturday will be booked, unless I find a new chaperone.

Sunday, I get to church 90 minutes early to practice the music, rehearse the choir, and then play the service. Sunday night is my first Edgewater Singers practice.

Some weeks it's even worse. Then there's travel for work; a two-week trip comes up soon.

Motion

Not much sticks to a surface in motion and nothing sinks in. I've been spinning so fast that not even God can penetrate. Is it possible to go faster than the speed of God? Even in church, my mind races so with weekday tasks and responsibilities that I can only feel my self, not God.

Singers

Diane is resigning as director of the Edgewater Singers, effective in May, when she and David will move to the house they are building in the country. Meanwhile she'll conduct the fall and spring rehearsals and concerts.

The rest of us are going to discuss whether to dissolve or stay together; if the vote is to continue, we have to find a new director.

This could be an opportunity for me. If the group dissolves, I can retire gracefully, too. And even if it continues, someone else can take over the piano work. If Diane can give nine months' notice, so can I.

That would open up some space for grad school—32 Sunday nights of space, plus countless hours I wouldn't need to devote to practicing.

14 years I've played for the Singers. I joined them the same year the divorce from Maxwell was final. It was the first activity I embraced as I came out of my "who-me-get-divorced?" cocoon. Our rehearsals always end with wine and refreshments, so it meant that once a week I had a social engagement, a date of sorts.

I like being active and absorbed in life. I like making music. I hate saying no. But this "no" would let me say "yes" to a new path.

Notice

I told CSA I wouldn't host the vegetable drop
site next year. I'll announce at the Singers
meeting that I'd like to stop accompanying.

That's 12 months notice to the farm and
9 months notice to the singers. Not exactly
spontaneous . . . but responsible.

Cheap

A big emphasis in my old simplicity group was spending
less. Sometimes that meant buying less and sometimes
it meant buying *for* less.

It's always satisfying to get a good deal, but cheap
goods often make people cheap, as they are mistreated
or abused in order to keep the cost of production
down. Cheap strikes me as antithetical to the Christian
life. If, as children of God who are equally valued and
loved by God, we are commanded to love and respect one
another as God's children, why would we ever willingly
buy something whose production exploited others?

There's a young man in my Spanish class who is
studying business and economics in college. The other
day, doing our best to communicate in our second
language, our class discussed how big retailers affect
rural and small town economies. Jeremy kept saying,
"but it's efficient" and "it's effective." It was
impossible to get him to recognize, in either
language, the human cost of the "efficient" system.

Finally in frustration I leaned over, patted him on
the thigh, and said (badly, ungrammatically, but with
passion), "Someday you'll understand that life is
about a lot more than effectiveness and efficiency."
It was a patronizing gesture, but because I'm the age
of his mother, I'm sure it rolled right off.

On Not Owning a Car

Pros:

- No more $50 tickets because I left my car on the street on street cleaning day.
- No more moments when the car suddenly rolls to an inexplicable stop, and I wonder how to get Alex and me home and the car from wherever it is to the shop.
- No more kid carpools!
- No more $500 Visa charges for car repair.
- No more insurance payments.
- No worries about paying the rising price of gas.
- I make $200 a month by renting both of my garage spaces.
- More money in my budget for things we enjoy.
- Getting to ride my bicycle more.
- No car payment!
- No worries about someone scratching the paint or getting in an accident.

Cons:

- Can't throw my Christmas tree in the car and recycle it at the park.
- Can't drive to Wisconsin with bikes or skis in the back.
- When I'm late, I'm late.
- I have to plan ahead more. Goodbye, spontaneity.
- No car for Alex to learn to drive in.
- Have to rent cars for funerals.
- 50-pound bags of dog food are hard to get home.

Moving Day

October 1st is moving day, so this morning the alley was teeming with items left behind by folks changing residences. Barks and I passed two recliner chairs, a wooden table, a vintage kitchen chair, a bed frame, and a lot of junk: a broken futon frame and a stained futon, broken bookcases (particleboard, not real wood), busted laminated storage units of various kinds. An area rug was sticking out of my neighbor's can. On its side was taped a little note to prospective scavengers: "no good—cat odor." Is that true, I wonder? Would the odors resist dry cleaning?

Although I've cleaned up several rugs from the alley, a colleague claims that it isn't an option for everyone. To rescue a rug, you need to be able to lift it—something she can't do. Then you need to be able to carry it to your laundry room. If your building doesn't have a laundry, you need to get it to the laundromat or the dry cleaner. In short, it's too much schlepping for some people.

She's right, but I still get offended when people seem to prefer discarding something to just plain washing it. Isn't that wasteful?

October

I drank my coffee on the picnic table for a front-row view of the butterflies visiting the buddleia bush on their way south to Mexico. Meanwhile, when Jennifer and Bob and I sat on the back porch the other day drawing, I drew the buddleia.

Application

No wonder I never bothered to go to graduate school when I was young. Applying is such a big drag.

There are so many forms to fill out and so many details to dredge up. My SAT scores from 1974. My GRE scores from 1978. My GPA. Transcripts, of which there are quite a few. Essays to write. Samples of creative writing to submit. Recommendations to secure. It's all due by early November. I wish I had more time now, but I'm still the accompanist and still dragging those boxes of vegetables over to Sue's house at 10 at night. Only for three more weeks, though.

Score

When I worked at home, shaping a career took a back seat to parenting Alex. Four years into an office job, notions of ambition and accomplishment are overtaking me. A lot more of my identity is tied up in what I do all day. It's especially noticeable now that I'm having to let go of Alex.

The writer Anne Herbert tells a story in which ambition and accomplishment are the reasons why God expelled humans from the Garden of Eden. In the beginning, her story goes, God made a bunch of people because God wanted us to have fun and you need a bunch of people to have fun. Then God put everyone into a playground called Eden and told us to enjoy. We did, at first, but one day this snake told us that we would have more fun if we kept score, and gave an apple to the person who was best at playing.

Well, each of us thought we were the best, so we made up lots of rules to confirm who was best. We quit playing simple, silly games that were too hard to score. By the time God found out about this, we were spending more of our days working out the score than we were playing.

God kicked us out of the garden and said we couldn't come back until we stopped keeping score. Anyhow, God said, we were going to die anyway, so our scores wouldn't mean anything.

But, Herbert's story says, God was wrong. Now we spend all our days keeping score. We teach our children to score high and hope that they'll outscore us. For most of us, it's the idea of a rule-less, score-less Eden that makes us nervous. How would we know who was who and who was ahead? It's scoring that gives us meaning. "We're all very grateful to the snake," her story ends.

I'm ashamed to say I spend plenty of days wondering about my total life score.

Straw

Halloween is a big deal in this neighborhood.
Streets are blocked off to make it easier for
kids to trick or treat, and people decorate
their lawns and sit on their porches giving
away candy. Since Alex is all grown up now, I
took the young Sudanese boys from church trick
or treating. It was a marvelous evening—all
those kids, all those costumes, all that candy!

The boys haven't lived here long, but they ran
into plenty of classmates and teachers as we
made the rounds. It seemed like evidence that
they are settling in and getting to know
people. To their dad, it's not enough. "In
Africa, I would know everybody on the block by
now," he remarked as we were talking later. I
thought it was pretty good that they knew three
families on the block! My standards of
community aren't as high as I imagined.

Bales of straw that decorated porches are
ending up in the alley this week. Today I
brought home a bale to use to mulch the
flowerbeds. My friend Dan drove it home in his
truck. He was passing by when I found the bale,
and was glad to drive it home for me. It would
be way too heavy for my shopping cart.

iPod

"I have a confession to make," Alex told me
at the theater tonight. "I'm going to buy an
iPod. It's probably against your
principles."

It's not. The iPod makes sense to me. Why
not replace two shelves of CDs with a tiny
little gadget? It's simple, in its way.

Will someone beat him up and steal it? I
wondered. There was that rash of headlines
about iPod killings; risking your life for
a hip appliance sounds like a bad idea.

"No, that was in the days when the
headphones were bigger and more obvious.
Anyway, they are more common now," he
explained.

That's true. On the el, it seems everyone
but me is under headphones, swaying to their
own private sound track.

"You must have rubbed off on me, though,"
Alex mused. "My friends were really
surprised that I would buy one. They
couldn't believe it."

Computer

I need a technological upgrade, too. Since
I do most of my work in an office now, my home
computer is sadly out of date. It has no
working external disk drives; either I type
stuff into it, or e-mail myself files from
somewhere else.

With a new computer, I could unhook the fax
line (no one faxes anymore!) and use the money
I spend on two phone lines and dial-up service
to get DSL. If it were a laptop, I could work
in different places in my house or even sit
outside.

A new computer would definitely simplify
things, and I could finally stop wasting money
on bad Internet service and the extra phone
line. It's time that stops me, not money.
Finding the best model, buying upgraded
software, having someone move the software and
files to the new computer and install DSL for
me—what a chore.

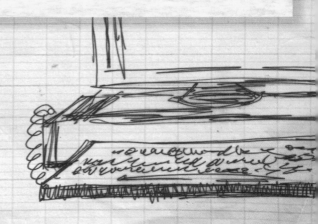

Online

Resodding the grass was easier than buying a new computer, because I know gardens. For me, computers and online services are like cars: I don't know what's under the hood. I don't feel equipped to make a good decision, so I'm not sure what step to take next.

Whereas Alex is at home with iPods, blogs, and personal Web pages, even computer games, although we never had a Nintendo. A young designer at work says, "You can live your life on MySpace." That's not where I live *my* life.

What will simple living mean to his generation?

Alex has absorbed a lot from his dad and me and our parents. Behind him are generations of cautious, frugal people who formed their living habits in response to immigration and world events.

"I'm good at waiting," my mom said recently when we were talking about this. "First there was the depression, and then all we heard was 'wait until the war is over.' What will happen when my generation is gone?"

From my generation comes this wisdom, from actress and writer Carrie Fisher who quips, "Instant gratification takes too long."

Thanksgiving

A very quiet holiday. I've been sick with a bad cold for six days, only getting out of bed to get water, soup, or another book. I had the strength to accept Val's invitation to dinner. Dick came too, and brought roses.

After supper Val asked for our help in choosing a coat. She couldn't decide in the store so she bought four of them and brought them home. One at a time she modeled them and asked for our feedback. We helped her pick one; now she'll return all the others. I'm so allergic to shopping, the idea of multiple trips makes me sneeze.

When Alex came home from celebrating Thanksgiving with his dad, he said, "I celebrated Thanksgiving three times, Mom. I gave thanks for my life with you, for my life with dad, and for my new autonomous life."

Buy Nothing Year

The day after Thanksgiving—when folks like me celebrate Buy Nothing Day!

I read about a group in the Bay Area that is vowing not to buy anything new next year except food, health and safety items, and underwear. Secondhand stuff is okay with them, so they look for stuff in thrift shops and online lists like freecycle.org.

What have I bought new this year that isn't food, pharmacy items, and underwear?

- 18 new books (another dozen used)
- Two pairs of shoes and two tank tops

- a Loveland Ski Area shirt (a souvenir for Alex of our college trip to Colorado)
- phone cards for the Brazilian exchange students
- invitations to Alex's graduation party
- an inexpensive 35-millimeter camera
- six rolls of film
- windshield wipers for Kevin, in thanks for the six times he lent me his car
- a pastel drawing by a North Dakota artist
- a framed photograph by a Chicago artist
- 10 Chinese shoulder bags for Christmas presents (left over from my denomination's big summer event)
- photo storage sleeves, and some supplies for the scrapbook I'm going to make, someday
- 100 issues of the *New York Times*

Supplies for the building:
- two new showerheads
- a tub strainer
- parts for the first floor dishwasher
- keys for the new garage tenant
- a new sink and toilet for the basement bathroom
- paint for the basement bathroom
- sod and flagstones for the backyard
- peat moss and grass seed
- weather stripping for two doors.

That's it, really.

This group has pledged to stop buying new stuff in order to stop killing our environment. I agree with their experiment. I'm sure I could cut back even further on buying new stuff—but I want to read the newspaper, and when a tenant needs keys, he needs keys.

Bill

My brother-in-law Bill died, after a long fight with brain cancer. We didn't always get along, but there was one thing I always appreciated: his unfailing interest in car sharing. He thought it was the coolest thing that I had sold my car and lived without one. To Bill, car sharing was a great concept. Whenever Alex and I showed up for a family party, he wanted to see the car we drove in. He gave I-Go promotional material to his employees, because he thought their families could benefit. I was always tickled that car sharing had such an unlikely ally in the head of a four-car family in the heart of the car-dependent suburbs.

For the visitation and the funeral cortege, service, and luncheon, I drove a shiny white I-Go Honda. It was an honor.

Struggle

Being overscheduled intensifies the struggle between being a human being and getting it all done.

When I'm trying to get it all done, I'm edgy and snappy. "Not pleasant" is a polite way of putting it.

Worried and preoccupied, I can't respond as one human to another. It's all about utility—what I have to do for others, what they can do for me.

Dick sprains his ankle and needs my help getting to the hospital, and I fret about missing a morning of work and blowing a deadline. My brother-in-law dies, and what strikes me first is the inconvenience of having to set everything aside to attend a funeral.

Of course I took Dick to the hospital, and Alex and I spent two days at Bill's wake, funeral, internment, and luncheon. But something is wrong when a life is packed so tightly there's no room to be gracious about life's emergencies—no room to be a human being to someone else.

God's Work

A story heard at work today: A hard-working pastor's wife complained when he came home late at night, "I can never get mad at you because you are doing God's work!"

That rang true. The sense of doing God's work makes it hard for folks like me who work for churches or the church-related organizations to take a break—and hard for their families to ask them to stop. But even God's people need to slow down. I'm trying.

Multitask

Pay bills while you're watching TV. Catch up on phone calls from your car. Standard advice in the women's magazines I read in the bathtub, but it doesn't work for me. When I try to multitask, my concentration vanishes. Especially when one of the things I'm trying to do simultaneously involves someone else. Playing computer solitaire when phone conversations drag on, for example. Spaces start to appear in my sentences. I say "uh huh" a lot. It's insulting, and I shouldn't do it.

The whole notion of multitasking assumes that we can be endlessly more efficient. It never stops to ask the question, should I be this busy?

Birdhouses

My brother John called. He built 20 birdhouses for kids to paint at his daughter Lily's birthday party. Last year they had the guests make fairy wands out of sticks, pipe cleaners, and ribbon.

They're big project people, John and Nina. "When I prune the apple trees, I can't burn anything, because Nina knows we can use it somehow," he said.

John is a carpenter, a teacher, and a student. He's stressed by his schedule, too.

"I've got project after project due," he said. "It's like airplanes stacked up and waiting to land. I'm the air traffic controller, deciding which project lands when."

He had hoped to rest a little over Thanksgiving, but besides the holiday meal they celebrated Nina's birthday and Lily's birthday. "It was supposed to be a break, but it wasn't," he said.

Yes

Grad school said yes. I start in January. I'm excited *and* scared.

Ten Percent

Here's a shocking fact: most cars sit idle 90 percent of the time.

Is there any other item we pay so much for and use so little? Imagine if we only lived in our houses 10 percent of the time and spent the other 90 worrying about where they were parked. What if we only ate 10 percent of the groceries we brought home or wore 10 percent of our clothes?

It makes our fascination with cars look like a fetish. Take my neighbor with the Lincoln Navigator that he won't park more than 30 yards from his apartment. Many is the night I see him idling in front of the fire plug, waiting for someone to pull out so he can pull in. His car is probably occupied 15 percent of the time, because he invests 5 percent looking for the perfect parking space.

It's a strong argument for sharing cars—except, as my friend Rose points out about her two-driver, one-car family, they always need the car the same 10 percent of the time.

Yard Cleanup

A good day in the garden at the end of a week that was really, really, really full. *Overload* full. It's kind of fun to be in a sweatshirt after several months of short sleeves and get dirty tearing out annuals and tossing them in the compost, mulching the roses, raking leaves and getting the yard ready for winter.

A big pile of brush is growing on the stone patio. The buddleia and rose bush branches and spent raspberry canes are too big to put into the compost and too hard for me to chop up by hand. I wish I could feed everything into a chipper shredder and end up with small compostable pieces.

I don't want to own one. I want *access* to a chipper shredder. One that several people, like the block club, could own in common and share.

It makes so much more sense than investing in a big tool I would use twice a year. I read recently that the average power tool gets used only 30 minutes in a lifetime. That's true of my tool box. My drill, my power sander, my Milwaukee SawZall sit idle almost always. Yet we buy and store them anyway!

I don't want to share my toaster or my toothbrush, but I'd gladly share a chipper.

More Sharing

I surveyed about three dozen friends and colleagues by e-mail to see what they wished they could share instead of own.

Most people listed outdoor equipment. Chippers got a lot of votes, probably because using it as an example biased the survey, but snowblowers got the most. Some people share them already. Kerry and Jim, former members of my church, said, "We share a snow blower with two of our neighbors. Ellie, who is 72, lets us use hers and then one of us helps her with her yard."

Other outdoor tools people wish they could share:

- rototiller
- a tall extension ladder to clean out the gutters (several votes)

- "I could use a power washer a couple times a year to wash off my siding and my deck."
- a wood splitter
- tillers
- portable sump pump
- weed trimmer
- chainsaw
- a trailer for hauling things
- pole limb saw
- wheelbarrow
- camping equipment
- barbeque grill ("We share ours with the neighbors")

Inside, people mostly mentioned kitchen equipment:

- canning equipment
- cake platters and serving platters
- punch bowl
- roasting pan

Other indoor items:
a card table and chairs,
a rug shampooer, a crib
and high chair for
visiting grandchildren,
and inflatable mattresses
for visiting friends
and family.

Terri said maybe she could
share a vegetable and herb
garden. Rochelle would
like to share lawn care
and meal preparation.
Liz would like to share
a video camera with
another family with small
children. Three voted
for cars.

Maureen says, "I'll share
anything but men!"

Chipper

Before work, I mowed the lawn. Nearby was a whir,
the sound of a powerful engine doing something
serious—a truck from the city's Bureau of
Forestry, trimming trees and chipping the branches!

I walked two loads of brush to the corner, and
had it all chipped for free. The brush is all
responsibly disposed of, and off my patio.
My lucky day!

Teachers

After I read today that the average college student accrues more than $2,700 in credit card debt while in school, and that about 10 percent owe more than $7,000, I wondered whether Alex was merrily charging pizzas with a credit card issued by some unscrupulous company.

"No, and don't worry about it," he said when I called to ask. "My high school did a pretty good job on that. Before we graduated, we had to go a special meeting where we talked about all sorts of things related to college. The counselors did a little skit that emphasized the danger of running up a credit card bill like it's not real money. Afterwards, we discussed it. And our teachers took every opportunity to warn us about it, like in math, when we studied interest, or in Mrs. Fritsch's class, when she went on one of her tangents."

He's lucky that his teachers were mentors, and I'm lucky that he always listens to his teachers. Way back in Montessori School, he listened when his kindergarten teacher warned them about Nintendos. He listened so carefully that when his dad tried to give him one for his sixth birthday, he refused to accept it, to the amazement of everyone.

His answer reassured me. And then a little later I noticed, as I was paying my own Visa bill, that my credit limit is $37,300.

I owe $930.57, most of it an airplane ticket I'll be reimbursed for when my next work trip is over. But don't worry, says Visa. I can still charge $36,369.

Imagine the trouble I'd be in if I took that seriously!

Shrink-Wrap

Walking with Barks, I saw a shrink-wrapped
SUV on a parking slab. Really, shrink-wrapped!
Completely slathered in plastic, so no one could
get in or out of the car.

How did it get there?

Was it dropped off?

Why is it wrapped up?

Take Two

The shrink-wrapped SUV is still there. Two days, now.
It's not winter. No bad weather is in the forecast.
It's parked off the street, where no one can scratch
or ding it.

It's funny to imagine why this is happening.

Maybe it's a new storage trend, like having containers
dropped off on your lawn.

Like a facial masque, maybe there is a beneficial
ointment slathered under the plastic.

Maybe it's a message from a finance company. First we
shrink-wrap, then we repossess.

Jan

Just as I was taking my omelet off the stove, my
friend Jan called from New York City. She was
standing on the subway platform near the Brooklyn
Botanic Garden and had 20 minutes before her train
came. About every four minutes our conversation was
interrupted by an express train, but we still
covered lots of ground. I liked the way her cell
phone helped us wedge a little friendship into our
separate days.

She had some advice for me, too, about my life
without Alex. She's in love, lately, but not very
confident about her relationship skills—the result
of so many years spent designing her life her way
and making all her decisions by herself. Enjoy your
independence, she said, but don't forget how to
live with other people.

Footprint

I keep hearing about ecological footprints—an assessment of how many resources we use to sustain our lives. So I spent about three minutes calculating mine at www.myfootprint.org

The average American ecological footprint is 24 acres. That means it takes 24 acres of resources to sustain the average American lifestyle.

Even without a car, even with compact fluorescent light bulbs, even eating lots of vegetables and walking everywhere, my ecological footprint is 17 acres. 17 acres to sustain me, every year!

"If everyone lived like you," the site scolded, "we would need 4.3 planets."

Jon Kabat Zinn says, "If you can't do something positive, why not simply avoid harming. If you can't help the earth, can you at least not harm it?"

I thought I was not harming the earth, but it looks like I was wrong.

Ouch

A menstrual period showed up this week. They're almost always unexpected now.

For two days, my body aches. It becomes a rubber band that someone is twisting. All my muscles and joints feel shorter, tighter, and achier. I spend time stretching and swallowing ibuprofen. I also lie down a lot—unusual for me.

Imagining, this week, that my body had a voice, I could hear it saying: "Anne, don't work us so hard, don't make us do so much, don't make us get up early for Spanish, don't make us go to Pilates, don't make us go to graduate school, please let us rest." Stina Kajsa would sniff at that and tell my body to get back to work. But with those little voices around me, the voices of my muscles and corpuscles and cells, I thought, hmm, I don't really have to take two graduate classes right away next quarter. I could just take one. So I dropped a class.

Then I had to write a little note to myself: the opposite of taking two classes is not indolence.

What drives me to overschedule and overwork are my own expectations. "I should do more," I tell myself when really I should just stop.

classes is not indolence. The opposite of taking two classes is not indolence. The opposite of taking two classes is not indolence. The opposite of taking two classes is not indolence. The opposite of taking two classes is not indolence. The opposite of taking two classes is not indolence.

Happy to Be Here

Today I looked around my church and thought, "I'm really glad to be here."

It's partly gratitude for being home after a weeklong work trip, and partly gratitude for just being alive—gratitude enhanced by the sadness of my brother-in-law Bill's death.

I don't often catch myself content. More often, I'm too worried about the next place I'm supposed to be or the tasks I feel I should be doing.

That was a dangerous frame of mind for me when Alex was little. It didn't take many weeks to discover that as a mom, I was best when I was fully present. If I was distracted and pressured, feeling like I should be doing something else, I was edgy and irritable. But if I was content to be with Alex, living at his pace, I could be a kind, imaginative mother.

That feeling of contentment breaks out at choir, too. Objectively speaking, you'd look at my crowded week and think: why not skip Wednesday night and just practice Sunday mornings? But the music we make together sustains and calms me. I enter those 90 minutes and stay there, glad.

After service, I stuck around and helped the choir decorate the sanctuary for Advent. First we had coffee, of course—but then we hung garlands, set up the tree, and talked. I felt happy to be there every single minute.

Feeling like I have to be in two places at the same time is a real joy killer. Could I bottle happy-to-be-here and take a whiff next time I hit an I'm-late-gotta-run moment?

Rutabagas

Late fall vegetables: so boring, so indestructible. Rutabagas, turnips, carrots, potatoes, squash: my heart sinks when I look at them. On the one hand, I know they'll last until January. On the other hand, by January I'll be really, really tired of them.

When the thrill of cooking fall's stews and soups wears off, I realize that winter food is here. It's comforting but bland. By January, bean soups with kale, baked squash, and fried potatoes will be a bore. I'll be dying to make a stir-fry with cilantro or eat at a Thai restaurant just for its sharp flavors.

I can tell that the other subscribers are getting bored now, too. They aren't as careful about picking up their orders. I have more to take to Sue. The boxes are much heavier and it's a major hassle for both of us, delivering all these pounds of food.

I did let the farm know I won't be hosting the drop site next year. I'm a little nostalgic already for boxes under the stairs—but when it takes two trips to drag the squash to Sue's house, I'm relieved by my decision.

Coat

I bought a new used coat today, a really
beautiful black coat made by Ralph Lauren. It's
cozy, roomy, and very warm. I can see I'll have
to attach the buttons a little more tightly, and
make a repair or two to the hem, but it was a
good deal at $35.

In the store, I felt a little offended at having
to pay so much. Then I thought: I haven't bought
a new winter coat since 1983, when I was young,
married, and new to Midwest winters. I probably
paid $130 for that coat. Since then, my coats
have been free because they've been handed down
by other people. So I can afford $35.

So far this year, I've spent $172.12 on clothing.
I bought a pair of sandals and some little flats
embroidered with rhinestones that I'll keep under
my desk and wear in the office on snowy days. I
bought two new tank tops plus two summer dresses
from the resale shop, a really nice skirt from
my neighbor Marianne's garage sale, and this
coat.

I needed a new coat; the last one had threadbare
elbows and a lining that was beyond repair. I've
got a couple of parkas (also hand-me-downs) for
cold Saturdays, but I needed something more
formal. This will do nicely.

I don't think I will need any more new clothes
for a while.

Birthday

I'm 49—a ridiculous age, insignificant and completely overshadowed by what's ahead. I'm about to spend 12 months replying, "I'll be 50 in December," when people ask my age.

Alex came home to celebrate. We walked to a new dessert place on Clark Street and split a huge and delicious slab of cake with ice cream. Afterwards we picked up Barks and walked over to the el stop, where he joined some schoolmates to attend a play. We stood around shivering on the cold snowy corner while we hugged goodbye. A girl trilled, "Oh, can we have hugs, too?" So I hugged them all. It was fun.

I'd like to mark 50 with a splashier event. But not too splashy! Not like the hiking trip I just read about, in which 13 women in their 50s spent four days traveling Inca Trail to Machu Picchu. They brought along real jam, real milk, real china, and real glassware: "Juice glasses, wineglasses, champagne flutes. We had 54 fleet porters to carry our astounding collection of essential and not-so-essential things, including our tents, down sleeping bags, two kitchen tents, two dining tents, two toilet tents, two massage tents, an oven (imagine!), 18 bottles of wine, several twenty-liter bottles of water with dispensers, and 800 pounds of food—including eggs, which perched atop a porter's load."

And camping is considered a simple living sort of activity!

Champagne flutes may be part of my 50th birthday celebration—but no porters. Definitely no porters.

186

Saturday, may 5, 1973

Dear Ingela,

Ingela Letter

A letter I sent to my cousin Ingela in Sweden in 1973...and she included in this year's Christmas letter. I was already too busy, and I was 16.

...summer is fast approaching... last week was beautiful- temperatures in the 80's, clear skies, a small breeze and a backyard full of people, including the johnsons. this week has been windier and cooler the last two days partially...

Shopocalypse

Rev. Billy visited Michigan Avenue today. He isn't a pastor but a performance artist whose group is called "Church of Stop Shopping." His message: "We are addicted, conflicted, hypnotized, and consumerized. We've got to save Christmas from the shopocalypse!"

He and his "choir" of followers shouted, "Stop shopping! Start living!" Most people just marched right by and into the store.

to get a job this summer so I can begin saving for future items - college, an apartment, or things for in the future... and immediate expenses such as clothes and piano lessons.

I signed up to take a class in drama appreciation during the night session of summer school, and with all that plus things that go along with summer vacation I should be on my feet 25 hours a day, but I'll have a good time. no one else in this family has any special plans except that we have to go to washington to visit my uncle, and my mom wants to go to the grand canyon, but that would be so hot!

did you hear about our giant explosion here, when the roseville train yards caught fire and blew up all the bombs in the box cars? that was a scary day- janet barham (remember her? she lives on markham, she is a friend of mine and always at my house) and I went bicycle riding on some river trails and didn't know the distance between us and the yards, but those explosions were loud and very much closer to the trails than to our houses. all day long I was expecting the city to be blown up, for the end of the world to come. that sounds morbid but it was

187

"Ramadan Ritual: Fast Daily, Pray, Head to the Mall"

The New York Times: "Once an ascetic month of fasting, prayer and reflection on God, Ramadan has gradually taken on the commercial trappings of Christmas and Hanukkah, from the hanging lights that festoon windows to the Ramadan greeting cards and Ramadan sales and advertising campaigns that have become the backbone of commerce for the month.

"For advertisers, Ramadan is like a 30-day Super Bowl weekend." TV channels in Muslim countries broadcast their best programming and marketers spend half their annual ad budget, because they will reach people who are home in the evening enjoying *iftar*, the after-sundown feast.

"People have taken this month to be a month of shopping," says one sheik from Dubai. Sounds like it's a month of food, too, because women get very competitive about the dishes they serve. "Ramadan has become a month where people exercise gluttony," says one man who objected to the trend. There weren't any quotes from people making choices that resisted it. I wonder what the Egyptian version of simple living looks like?

Cheer

The Edgewater Singers show and party was last night—lots of good food and company, and a late night sing-a-long—but there's still more Christmas music to practice with the church choir, and I'm playing Christmas Eve, Christmas Day, and New Year's weekend services. I'll play for the party at work, the St. Lucia festival at the Swedish American Museum, and two more Advent services.

Music plunges me into Advent and Christmas. Being a musician, I'm inside and outside of the experience at the same time. I love the sense of creating something that engages others, but it's the audience or congregation who get the full effect.

Tree

This year my Christmas tree is recycled!

It came from Diane and David, who left town the day after their post-Christmas-concert party. When she told me a few days earlier that they were taking their tree down, I asked for it. They dumped it in my back yard yesterday.

Of course, this is the kind of thing that makes some of my friends shake their heads and think, "She's completely around the bend." But I think it's a win-win situation. I saved $60, some time (we didn't have to walk over and select one, and then carry it home), and some other poor tree's life. And it looks wonderful!

Wanting

"Wants" is a charming and very short Grace Paley story about a woman who encounters her ex-husband one day. They talk briefly about their marriage.

"I wanted a sailboat, he said. But you didn't want anything. . . . You'll always want nothing.

"I felt extremely accused. Now it's true, I'm short of requests and absolute requirements. But I do want *something*. I want, for instance, to be a different person."

That is, says the narrator, someone who turns library books in on time, who changes the school system, who ends the war, who is married forever to one person.

Most of my wants also have less to do with goods and more to do with ambitions and characteristics.

In our culture, where every ad aims to make us want more, wanting less is countercultural.

Consumers

"Probably the worst thing that has happened to our understanding of reality has been our acceptance of ourselves as consumers. Our greed is consuming the planet, so that we may quite easily kill this beautiful earth by daily pollution without ever having nuclear warfare. Sex without love consumes, making another person an *object*, not a *subject*. Can we change our vocabulary and our thinking? To do so may well be a matter of life and death. Consumers do not understand that we must live not by greed and self-indulgence but by observing and contemplating the wonder of God's universe as it is continually being revealed to us."

From *Glimpses of Grace: Daily Thoughts and Reflections*, by Madeline L'Engle and Carole F. Chase.

Parallel Play

Alex came home to help put up the tree yesterday. We set it in that Christmas tree stand I found in the alley last January, the one that still had its price tag. Instead of teetering on four legs like the old stand, this has a wide plastic base and can't be tipped over. Much easier, much more stable—an all-round welcome innovation.

As we strung lights and placed ornaments, we talked about his school, my work, our family. The shared activity helped conversation came easily.

We were like two little kids playing side by side, except this was a grownup version of parallel play.

Skiing has been another form of parallel play for us. On the lift between runs or standing at the top of the hill, it's easy to share news and feelings. But relaxed,

spontaneous conversations are rarer now that Alex is home so infrequently. When he does visit, my attempts at a mother-to-son, so-tell-me-what's-new-with-you conversation don't work. Too much pressure, I guess. My thanks to the Christmas tree for its diversion.

Parties

Alex came with me to a holiday party. After mingling halfheartedly with folks we see once a year at this party we filled up our plates, grabbed two chairs, and talked to one another. Alex had lots to say about the classes he has finished, the subjects he is studying. He would like to study philosophy and told me why. Our long conversation was the best part about the evening.

There's still one more party—an open house on Thursday night. I think I'll say no and stay home. It's too close to Christmas and I'm running out of steam.

No Car

I asked Kevin what life is like now that he's been without a car for three months.

"I walk more, of course," he said. "And my life is more regularized because I get the 6:40 bus every morning instead of leaving when I feel like it. I read a study that said a steady routine is actually healthier than all the running around I used to do. And I do more things in the immediate neighborhood instead of drive someplace else. The other day, I walked down the street for a cup of tea at the Urban Tea Lounge."

Kevin's apartment is opposite soccer fields, on the edge of a big park. Because street parking places are hard to find, he often used to leave the car on a street in the park. Chicago is pretty safe, but dark, deserted sidewalks in parks aren't, and once, walking home at night, he was held up by a man with a gun. So I ventured that since the bus drops him off right in front of his apartment, he's actually safer coming home.

"That's right. And I don't worry any more about whether someone is trying to break into my car or steal it out of the park."

What about getting to Wisconsin to see his family? "The train and bus work fine."

Christmas Presents

Alex says what's depressing about giving Christmas presents to his cousins and aunts is feeling that we have to give something, but not knowing enough about the recipients to really buy something nice or appropriate.

Alex takes after his dad, a genius gift giver. Both of them think long and hard about the recipient. For Ben's 19th birthday, Alex burned 19 CDs, because all of Ben's CDs had been destroyed and he wanted music. For Samantha, he filled a Tonka truck with M&Ms. (That one made my friends sigh.) He and his friend Rachael from Holden exchange thoughts on cassette tapes. To give her a flavor of Chicago, he captured the roar of a Blue Line train coming into a station.

Alex and his friends are so young, so excited about each other and the world. They're on an upward curve of celebration and despair; I'm on the downward, been-there-done-that curve. Because they get to know one another so intently, so intensely, they can create or select gifts that perfectly suit the recipient.

I, on the other hand, bought the same present for every woman on my list. Efficient, but hardly personal. I wish I could capture the enthusiasm and perceptiveness of Alex and his friends and really think deeply about people and their gifts.

Ideas

A few ideas for giving presents without participating in the 'shopocalypse':

With 10 kids and 23 grandchildren, Kevin's family can't possibly give each other presents, so every Christmas they have a drawing. Everyone spends the next 11 months making or assembling a gift for the name they draw. The year Kevin's mother drew his name she made him a quilt. This year he is giving his niece a Chicago-themed present. He collected Chicago-made products like Lemonheads and Tootsie Rolls, and he packed them (plus some tickets to a show) in a sturdy cardboard box from a Chicago tortilla manufacturer.

They also circulate a painting called "Santa around the World." It started as a blank blue canvas with the tail end of Santa's hat and sleigh disappearing at the far left side. Now each family member who gets it must add something to it before passing it on. One brother added Mt. Kilimanjaro the year he visited Tanzania. Another family added the Eiffel Tower after a visit to Paris. When Kevin had it, he trimmed the top edge with fabrics from around the world. They all love it, and it makes them laugh.

Senses of humor are in short supply in my family—all those serious Swedes! But I've tried to pare back on giving things and give donations instead.

I'm not much on homemade presents, but when Alex was little, I made him a puppet theater out of a computer box. I covered it with bright red and yellow Contact paper, sewed little red-and-white striped curtains, and included a few hand puppets. He and his friends loved getting behind the curtain and making the puppets talk. That was my favorite gift to him, and he barely remembers it.

ALEX THEATRE

Serendipity

Shopping on Clark Street last night, I saw my friends Jane and Jose sitting at a window table at Andie's Restaurant. I dragged my cart (loaded with Christmas beer for my nephews and former father-in-law) into the restaurant, parked it next to the coat rack, and joined them. We spent a wonderful hour catching up over wine and appetizers, watching snow fall.

Wigilia

Another year, another Christmas Eve at my former in-laws, where we celebrate *Wigilia*, the Polish version of Christmas Eve.

The best part of the *Wigilia* is at the beginning, when we exchange *opłateks*, delicate oblong wafers imprinted with an image of the Virgin and Child. Everyone pairs off and holds out their *opłateks* to each other. As I give the other person wishes for the coming year— wishes for good health, discernment, help in a tough time—I break off pieces of the wafer. Then the other person makes wishes for me, and breaks pieces from my wafer.

It's deep and emotional. Tears flow as good times are remembered or losses are reviewed. The losses are mounting: my sister-in-law's husband died in 2001 of a brain tumor at 50; Alex's Grandma Dell died in January 2004 of breast cancer; and my sister-in-law Barb's husband Bill, just 52, died of lung and brain cancer the day after Thanksgiving.

The awkwardness of my position as ex-daughter-in-law, ex-sister-in-law melts away during this ritual. I'm blessed to be there, looking into the eyes of my ex-but-still-in-laws and blessing them for the year to come. Then there's the nine-course Polish meal, similar to Swedish

Christmas Eve dinners in that most of the food is beige: herring, barley and mushroom soup, potatoes, *pierogi*, *nalishniki*, some shrimp. My sisters-in-law work hard to keep this ritual going since their mother died, but looking around the table tonight, I thought that only one, maybe two of the eight grandchildren will take this menu into the next generation.

After cookies and coffee, Santa comes, and the evening starts to go downhill. Piles of presents appear. Countless rolls of wrapping paper are torn off and thrown away. All that has been intimate and sacred vanishes in the frenzy. Alex and I stop being participants; we exchange one or two presents with each other and then watch the goings-on.

Our gifts are small—beer, chocolate oranges, trinkets I've picked up in my travels for work. Our family gift, a goat or pig destined for a Heifer project in Poland, is announced in a modest gift card that, compared to the boxes flying around, seems puny and forgettable. So many gifts are exchanged in those 45 minutes, it's hard to imagine any one gift standing out.

It's easy to see why five million extra tons of trash are produced between Thanksgiving and New Year—and why everyone marches straight back to the store on the 26th to return and exchange gifts. It's hard to dream up one thoughtful present at a time. How can we dream up 12 or 15?

Later

Last night I played for the Christmas Eve service and this morning I played for Christmas. I was so tired—as usual, we got home from the family party at 2:00 am—I had a little meltdown, sitting at the organ playing yet another Christmas carol. (I've been playing them since September, really, when the Edgewater Singers started practicing!)

Why do I need to be everything to everyone? I wondered. Playing back-to-back services, rushing out to the suburbs for Christmas Eve, getting up and cooking breakfast for Alex before he left for his dad's, playing another service, and now I'm hosting a Christmas dinner for folks from church like me who are loose ends. Fortunately two other women are sharing in the cooking and decorating, and the dozen people we expected have dwindled down to seven. It will be delicious, but I'm really, really tired. And the turkey is way too big; I'll have piles of leftovers. Alex won't be around to help eat them, because he leaves in two days for Holden, where he'll volunteer for three more weeks.

This is when I feel most caught. On the one hand, I'm absorbed in a life filled with people and connection, music and meaning. On the other hand, I'm truly exhausted.

Grad school starts the first week of January. If I'm truly going to open up new possibilities in writing, I've got to eliminate more. In six months I'll be finished with the Edgewater Singers. I won't host vegetables next summer. Meanwhile, I'm still overscheduled. I have to pare down more—say no more—to say yes to this new challenge.

I'd like to go from being busy—surely my default mode—to being wise.

December 26

Most of my presents came from the neighborhood—
I like shopping locally—and or come from my
church or my job. For my sister's boys, Alex and
I pass along a toy that's in good shape. They
have so much already, and they're still young
enough to be impressed by what Alex owned, being
in the admiring-big-cousin-Alex stage. We've
passed along a beautiful mancala set, some easy
reader books, and the all-time favorite, old
sheets of press type left over from the days when
desktop publishing programs were an impossible
dream. Julian, Jonathan and John's daughter Lily
can rub it onto paper to make signs or onto blank
books to make stories. They love the stuff. It's
gone now, though: this year we distributed the
final inventory.

All told, our Christmas expenses of $320.52
covered gifts for about two dozen family members
plus groceries for Christmas dinner, a wreath for
the door (which I dolled up with extra pine cones
and ribbons from the basement closet), postage for
cards and packages, and a tip for the milkman.

198

Quiet

Finally, a moment to sit on the sofa and read in front of the tree. Alex used to have a Christmas season overnight with my friend Susan's kids. All three kids would lie on the sleeper sofa gazing at the twinkling tree until they fell asleep. I can feel a little of that sleepy peacefulness now.

Single Bed

New Year's Eve. Alex has gone to Holden for three weeks, but all the beds upstairs and down are full of out-of-towners here for our very good friend's very big 50th birthday party tonight.

Mary and Ricardo get my bedroom; I'm staying in Alex's single bed.

After my divorce, my mother wanted me to buy a single bed. Why did I need a double bed now that my marriage was over? All that space made her nervous.

There was so much pressure on me to apologize—to take up less space, to ask for less, to generally shrink into the diminished role of divorced mom and sorry about it. I didn't want to shrink, but I did, a little, at first, sorting through stuff, selling or giving things away, challenging myself to find ways to cut down expenses. Shrinking was a reflexive response to being injured.

But I kept the double bed and bought that big Volvo wagon. Even when I was hurt, the extra space seemed full of possibilities.

Contracting and expanding has pretty much been my rhythm ever since. Every place I chose to cut back, something else has been able to expand:

- Lower expenses, more ease in the world.
- Less TV, more time for friends and music and thinking.
- Lower car expenses, more money for donations, opera, and the new theater subscription I got with Alex.
- No car, less behind-the-wheel stress, greater creativity about transportation—and much sharper crossword puzzle skills.

This year my heart has contracted as Alex has started leaving our nest. I'm so sad that this part of our life together is closing, that the companionship I've taken for granted is changing. Since September, he has spent exactly one night here, and that was Christmas Eve. (He spent Christmas night with his dad.) All the other evenings, he has returned to his dorm room. Which is one reason why he wanted to stay in Chicago: so he could wake up in a place of his own, without wondering which parent's house he went to next.

This is a very, very painful contraction, but deep inside, I can feel the seeds of the next expansion. My heart is learning to embrace the concerns of three generations at once: Alex, launching; me, relaunching in midlife; aging neighbors like Dick, packing for the final journey. Some long-time activities like accompanying the Edgewater Singers and hosting vegetables, PTA meetings and report card pickup days, are going away. In their place, graduate classes start in two weeks—a door to something I can't even imagine.

This evening's six guests make me glad I still have my building, but my space and belongings will start to contract again soon.

Maybe I'll follow the example of the couple that is eliminating 10 percent of their possessions every year for the next ten years. I'm such a poor mathematician, I thought that meant they would own nothing at the end of the decade. Wrong. They'll just own a lot less, opening new possibilities for them. Who knows what paring down even more will let me do?

Like labor, all this contracting and expanding brings birth. It already has, and it will continue to. For every stingy Stina Kajsa moment, I savor three or four rich Lydia moments.

In my 50th year, God, may
I want less *and* more. Less
stuff, less stress, fewer
misplaced, self-induced
demands. Less greed, more
contentment. More time
with Alex, family, and
friends. More moments on
the porch. More hours in
your company, God. More
time to practice being
human, so I can prepare
for the big goodbyes
coming up.

Keep my heart open, and
teach me how to prevent my
stuff and my schedule from
closing me off from
others. In less, help me
find more—more space to
love the people you've
graced me with, more
willingness to build your
culture, more courage to
say yes.

Happy New Year.